First World War
and Army of Occupation
War Diary
France, Belgium and Germany

2 DIVISION
Headquarters, Branches and Services
Commander Royal Artillery
1 November 1915 - 30 November 1915

WO95/1316/2

The Naval & Military Press Ltd
www.nmarchive.com
Published in association with The National Archives

Published by

The Naval & Military Press Ltd

Unit 10 Ridgewood Industrial Park,

Uckfield, East Sussex,

TN22 5QE England

Tel: +44 (0) 1825 749494

www.naval-military-press.com

www.nmarchive.com

This diary has been reprinted in facsimile from the original. Any imperfections are inevitably reproduced and the quality may fall short of modern type and cartographic standards.

© **Crown Copyright**
Images reproduced by permission of The National Archives, London, England, 2015.

Contents

Document type	Place/Title	Date From	Date To
Heading	2nd Div R.A.H.Q. War Diary November 1915		
War Diary	Bethune (47)	01/11/1915	30/11/1915
Miscellaneous	Daily Ammunition Return	01/11/1915	01/11/1915
Miscellaneous	Daily Diary	01/11/1915	01/11/1915
Miscellaneous	A Form Messages And Signals		
Miscellaneous	Hostile Shelling		
Miscellaneous	2nd Division Artillery Orders Brigadier-General G.H. Sanders, D.S.O., Comdg. R.A., 2nd Divn.	01/11/1915	01/11/1915
Miscellaneous	A Form Messages And Signals		
Miscellaneous	Daily Diary	02/11/1915	02/11/1915
Miscellaneous	Daily Ammunition Return	02/11/1915	02/11/1915
Miscellaneous	2nd Division Artillery Orders by Brigadier-General G.H. Sanders, D.S.O., Comdg. R.A., 2nd Divn.	02/11/1915	02/11/1915
Miscellaneous	A Form Messages And Signals		
Miscellaneous	Daily Diary	03/11/1915	03/11/1915
Miscellaneous	A Form Messages And Signals		
Miscellaneous	Daily Ammunition Return	03/11/1915	03/11/1915
Miscellaneous	2nd Division Artillery Orders by Brigadier-General G.H. Sanders, D.S.O., Comdg. R.A., 2nd Divn.	03/11/1915	03/11/1915
Miscellaneous	R.A. 2nd Div Positions	04/11/1915	04/11/1915
Miscellaneous	A Form Messages And Signals		
Miscellaneous	Daily Diary	04/11/1915	04/11/1915
Miscellaneous	Daily Ammunition Return	04/11/1915	04/11/1915
Miscellaneous	2nd Division Artillery Orders by Lieut-Colonel C.R.P. Parry, Comdg. R.A., 2nd Division	04/11/1915	04/11/1915
Miscellaneous	Daily Diary	05/11/1915	05/11/1915
Miscellaneous	A Form Messages And Signals		
Miscellaneous	No. 1/R.A.S 105-9	02/11/1915	02/11/1915
Miscellaneous	Daily Ammunition Return	05/11/1915	05/11/1915
Miscellaneous	2nd Division Artillery Orders by Lieut-Colonel C.R.P. Parry, Comdg. R.A., 2nd Division	05/11/1915	05/11/1915
Miscellaneous	Daily Diary	06/11/1915	06/11/1915
Miscellaneous	A Form Messages And Signals		
Miscellaneous	Daily Ammunition Return	06/11/1915	06/11/1915
Miscellaneous	2nd Division Artillery Orders by Lieut-Colonel C.R.P. Parry, Comdg. R.A., 2nd Division	06/11/1915	06/11/1915
Miscellaneous	Daily Diary	07/11/1915	07/11/1915
Miscellaneous	A Form Messages And Signals		
Miscellaneous	2nd Division Artillery Observing Stations	07/11/1915	07/11/1915
Miscellaneous	Daily Ammunition Return	07/11/1915	07/11/1915
Miscellaneous	2nd Division Artillery Orders by Lieut-Colonel C.R.P. Parry, Comdg. R.A., 2nd Division	07/11/1915	07/11/1915
Miscellaneous	Daily Diary	08/11/1915	08/11/1915
Miscellaneous	A Form Messages And Signals		
Miscellaneous	Daily Ammunition Return	08/11/1915	08/11/1915
Miscellaneous	2nd Division Artillery Orders by Lieut-Colonel C.R.P. Parry, Comdg. R.A., 2nd Division	08/11/1915	08/11/1915
Miscellaneous	Daily Diary	09/11/1915	09/11/1915
Miscellaneous	A Form Messages And Signals		
Miscellaneous	Daily Diary	14/11/1915	14/11/1915

Miscellaneous	Daily Ammunition Return	09/11/1915	09/11/1915
Miscellaneous	2nd Division Artillery Orders by Lieut-Colonel C.R.P. Parry, Comdg. R.A., 2nd Division	09/11/1915	09/11/1915
Miscellaneous	Daily Diary	10/11/1915	10/11/1915
Miscellaneous	A Form Messages And Signals		
Miscellaneous	2nd Division No. G.S. 711/1	09/11/1915	09/11/1915
Miscellaneous	Daily Ammunition Return	10/11/1915	10/11/1915
Miscellaneous	2nd Division Artillery Orders by Lieut-Colonel C.R.P. Parry, Comdg. R.A., 2nd Division	10/11/1915	10/11/1915
Miscellaneous	Daily Diary	11/11/1915	11/11/1915
Miscellaneous	A Form Messages And Signals		
Miscellaneous	R.A. 2nd Divn Position	11/11/1915	11/11/1915
Miscellaneous	Daily Ammunition Return	11/10/1915	11/10/1915
Miscellaneous	2nd Division Artillery Orders by Lieut-Colonel C.R.P. Parry, Comdg. R.A., 2nd Division	11/11/1915	11/11/1915
Miscellaneous	Daily Diary	12/11/1915	12/11/1915
Miscellaneous	A Form Messages And Signals		
Miscellaneous	Daily Diary	13/11/1915	13/11/1915
Operation(al) Order(s)	2nd Division Operation Order No. 74	11/11/1915	11/11/1915
Miscellaneous	March Table Issued With 2nd Div. Operation Order No 74		
Miscellaneous	A Form Messages And Signals		
Miscellaneous	Daily Ammunition Return	12/11/1915	12/11/1915
Miscellaneous	2nd Divisional Artillery Orders by Lieutenant-Colonel C.R.P. Parry Commanding R.A. 2nd Divn	12/11/1915	12/11/1915
Miscellaneous	A Form Messages And Signals		
Miscellaneous	Daily Ammunition Return	13/11/1915	13/11/1915
Miscellaneous	2nd Division Artillery Orders by Lieut-Colonel C.R.P. Parry, Commanding R.A. 2nd Division.	13/11/1915	13/11/1915
Map	Map		
Miscellaneous	General Information 164th Bde R.F.A.	14/11/1915	14/11/1915
Miscellaneous	2nd Division No. G.S. 711/2	14/11/1915	14/11/1915
Miscellaneous	Daily Ammunition Return	14/11/1915	14/11/1915
Miscellaneous	Daily Diary	15/11/1915	15/11/1915
Miscellaneous	A Form Messages And Signals		
Miscellaneous	Daily Ammunition Return	15/11/1915	15/11/1915
Miscellaneous	General Information	15/11/1915	15/11/1915
Miscellaneous	2nd Division Artillery Orders by Colonel A. Eardley Wilmot, Commanding R.A. 2nd Divn.	15/11/1915	15/11/1915
Miscellaneous	Daily Diary	16/11/1915	16/11/1915
Miscellaneous	A Form Messages And Signals		
Miscellaneous	Daily Ammunition Return	16/11/1915	16/11/1915
Miscellaneous	2nd Division Artillery Orders by Brigadier-General G.H. Sanders, Comdg. R.A., 2nd Divn.	16/11/1915	16/11/1915
Miscellaneous	2nd Division Artillery Summary	17/11/1915	17/11/1915
Miscellaneous	Adv. First Army	18/11/1915	18/11/1915
Miscellaneous	A Form Messages And Signals		
Miscellaneous	Daily Ammunition Return	17/11/1915	17/11/1915
Miscellaneous	2nd Division Artillery Orders by Brigadier-General G.H. Sanders, D.S.O., Comdg. R.A., 2/Divn.	17/11/1915	17/11/1915
Miscellaneous	Daily Ammunition Return	18/11/1915	18/11/1915
Miscellaneous	2nd Divisional Artillery Summary		
Miscellaneous	A Form Messages And Signals		
Operation(al) Order(s)	2nd Division Operation Order No. 75	18/11/1915	18/11/1915
Miscellaneous	March Table Issued With 2nd Division Operation Order No. 75 dated 18th November 1915	18/11/1915	18/11/1915

Miscellaneous	Daily Diary	22/11/1915	22/11/1915
Miscellaneous	D.A. 2nd Div	22/11/1915	22/11/1915
Miscellaneous	R.A 2nd Division	18/11/1915	18/11/1915
Operation(al) Order(s)	2nd Division Artillery Operation Order No. 7	19/11/1915	19/11/1915
Miscellaneous	2nd Division Artillery Summary	19/11/1915	19/11/1915
Miscellaneous	A Form Messages And Signals		
Miscellaneous	Daily Ammunition Return	19/11/1915	19/11/1915
Miscellaneous	2nd Division Artillery Orders by Brigadier-General G.H. Sanders, D.S.O., Comdg. R.A., 2nd Divn.	19/11/1915	19/11/1915
Miscellaneous	2nd Division No. G.S. 740	19/11/1915	19/11/1915
Miscellaneous	Report on Wirecutting 2nd Div. Work Ending 20/11/15	20/11/1915	20/11/1915
Miscellaneous	2nd Division Artillery Summary	20/11/1915	20/11/1915
Miscellaneous	Daily Ammunition Return	20/11/1915	20/11/1915
Miscellaneous	2nd Division Artillery Orders by Brigadier-General G.H. Sanders, D.S.O., Comdg. R.A., 2nd Divn.	20/11/1915	20/11/1915
Miscellaneous	2nd Division Artillery Operation Order No. 7 Amendment	20/11/1915	20/11/1915
Miscellaneous	2nd Division Artillery Summary	21/11/1915	21/11/1915
Miscellaneous	Daily Ammunition Return	21/11/1915	21/11/1915
Miscellaneous	2nd Division Artillery Orders by Brigadier-General G.H. Sanders, D.S.O., Comdg. R.A., 2nd Divn.	21/11/1915	21/11/1915
Miscellaneous	A Form Messages And Signals		
Miscellaneous	64th Brigade RFA	22/11/1915	22/11/1915
Miscellaneous	A Form Messages And Signals		
Miscellaneous	2nd Division Artillery Winter Traning	22/11/1915	22/11/1915
Miscellaneous	2nd Division Artillery Orders by Brigadier-General G.H. Sanders, D.S.O., Comdg. R.A., 2nd Divn.	22/11/1915	22/11/1915
Miscellaneous	Daily Diary	23/11/1915	23/11/1915
Miscellaneous	Brigade R.F.A. Daily Report	23/11/1915	23/11/1915
Miscellaneous	36 Brigade R.F.A. Daily Report	23/11/1915	23/11/1915
Miscellaneous	2nd Division Artillery Report 23rd November 1915	23/11/1915	23/11/1915
Miscellaneous	A Form Messages And Signals		
Heading	F14 3 6 K & B 88 18 H Q		
Miscellaneous	Daily Ammunition Return	23/11/1915	23/11/1915
Miscellaneous	2nd Division Artillery Orders by Brigadier-General G.H. Sanders, D.S.O., Comdg. R.A., 2nd Divn.	23/11/1915	23/11/1915
Miscellaneous	2nd D.A. Diary		
Miscellaneous	2nd Division Hostile Fire Report	24/11/1915	24/11/1915
Miscellaneous	Daily Ammunition Return	24/11/1915	24/11/1915
Miscellaneous	2nd Division Artillery Orders by Brigadier-General G.H. Sanders, D.S.O., Comdg. R.A., 2nd Divn.	24/11/1915	24/11/1915
Miscellaneous	Group Diary	25/11/1915	25/11/1915
Miscellaneous	Z Group Diary	25/11/1915	25/11/1915
Miscellaneous	2nd Division Hostile Fire Report	25/11/1915	25/11/1915
Miscellaneous	Daily Ammunition Return	25/11/1915	25/11/1915
Miscellaneous	2nd Division Artillery Orders by Brigadier-General G.H. Sanders, D.S.O., Comdg. R.A., 2nd Divn.	25/11/1915	25/11/1915
Miscellaneous	Z Group Diary	26/11/1915	26/11/1915
Miscellaneous	Group Diary	26/11/1915	26/11/1915
Miscellaneous	2nd Divisional Artillery Hostile Fire Report	26/11/1915	26/11/1915
Miscellaneous	A Form Messages And Signals		
Miscellaneous	Daily Ammunition Return	26/11/1915	26/11/1915
Miscellaneous	2nd Division Artillery Orders by Brigadier-General G.H. Sanders, D.S.O., Comdg. R.A., 2nd Divn.	26/11/1915	26/11/1915
Miscellaneous	Group Diary	27/11/1915	27/11/1915
Miscellaneous	Z Group Diary	27/11/1915	27/11/1915

Miscellaneous	2nd Divisional Artillery Hostile Fire Report	27/11/1915	27/11/1915
Miscellaneous	In Reply to 2nd Division G.S.746		
Miscellaneous	B.M. Inst. 36a	27/11/1915	27/11/1915
Miscellaneous	2nd Division No. G.S.759/1	27/11/1915	27/11/1915
Miscellaneous	A Form Messages And Signals		
Operation(al) Order(s)	2nd Divisional Artillery Operation Order No. 8	27/11/1915	27/11/1915
Miscellaneous			
Miscellaneous	Daily Ammunition Return	27/11/1915	27/11/1915
Miscellaneous	2nd Divisional Artillery Orders by Brigadier General G.H. Sanders D.S.O. Comdg R.A. 2nd Divn	27/11/1915	27/11/1915
Miscellaneous	Group Diary	28/11/1915	28/11/1915
Miscellaneous	Z Group Diary	28/11/1915	28/11/1915
Miscellaneous	2nd Divisional Artillery Hostile Fire Report	28/11/1915	28/11/1915
Miscellaneous	A Form Messages And Signals		
Miscellaneous	R.A. 2nd Division Situation	28/11/1915	28/11/1915
Miscellaneous	Daily Ammunition Return	28/11/1915	28/11/1915
Miscellaneous	Z Group Diary	29/11/1915	29/11/1915
Miscellaneous	Group Diary	29/11/1915	29/11/1915
Miscellaneous	2nd Divisional Artillery Hostile Fire Report	29/11/1915	29/11/1915
Miscellaneous	2nd Divisional Artillery Orders by Brigadier General G.H. Sanders D.S.O. Comdg R.A. 2nd Divn	29/11/1915	29/11/1915
Miscellaneous	Diary	30/11/1915	30/11/1915
Miscellaneous			
Miscellaneous	2nd Divisional Artillery Hostile Fire Report	30/11/1915	30/11/1915
Miscellaneous	R.A. 2nd Div	30/11/1915	30/11/1915
Miscellaneous	Headquarters 2nd Division	30/11/1915	30/11/1915
Miscellaneous	A Form Messages And Signals		
Miscellaneous	Headquarters 2nd Division	30/11/1915	30/11/1915
Miscellaneous	List Of Officers R.A. 2nd Division		
Miscellaneous	Daily Ammunition Return	30/11/1915	30/11/1915

Index

SUBJECT.

No.	Contents.	Date.
	2ND DIV. R.A., H.Q. — WAR DIARY, NOVEMBER, 1915	

Army Form C. 2118.

WAR DIARY
or
INTELLIGENCE SUMMARY.
(Erase heading not required.)

Instructions regarding War Diaries and Intelligence Summaries are contained in F.S. Regs., Part II. and the Staff Manual respectively. Title pages will be prepared in manuscript.

Hour, Date, Place	Summary of Events and Information	Remarks and references to Appendices
1.XI.15 BETHUNE (?)	Dull and light. No action of importance. Ammunition expenditure. Routine orders	1424 1425 1426
2.XI.15	N wind. Fair, light frosty frost. All quiet. 12th Division joined 1st Corps. Ammunition expenditure. Routine orders	1427 1428 1429 1430
3.XI.15	All quiet. Light frost. Enemy showed white flags and sent a deputation near the Cambrin road. We did not fire at request of Troops Bdes. issued on this subject. Section of 7th Howitzers Battery places under 2nd Bde. Ammunition expenditure. Routine orders	1431 1432 1433 1434

Army Form C. 2118

WAR DIARY
or
INTELLIGENCE SUMMARY.
(Erase heading not required.)

Hour, Date, Place	Summary of Events and Information	Remarks and references to Appendices
4.XI.15 BETHUNE (47)	All quiet. Postins Ammunition expenditure Routine Orders Lt. Genl. G.H. Sandars paid visit. Lt. Colonel Parry took Command.	1436 1437 1438
5.XI.15	Very quiet. H.M. wired O.C. impossible 7.30pm to 6.9 am Orders for concentration in trenches issued Ammunition expenditure Routine Orders	1440 1441 1442 1443
6.XI.15	Very quiet. Observation impossible all day. August Ammunition expenditure Routine Orders	1444 1445 1446

WAR DIARY
or
INTELLIGENCE SUMMARY.

(Erase heading not required.)

Army Form C. 2118

Hour, Date, Place	Summary of Events and Information	Remarks and references to Appendices
7.XI.15 BETHUNE (17)	Very misty. Light breeze all day. Not list of observing stations. Been formerly inconvenient to be undertaken. Ammunition return	1447 1448 1449 1450
8.XI.15	All quiet. Observation impossible 4.15pm to 7.15am. Not. Ammunition expenditure. Routine orders	1451 1452 1453
9.XI.15	Very clear. All quiet. Observation impossible 4.30pm to 7am. Ammunition expenditure. Routine orders	1454 1455 1456

Army Form C. 2118

WAR DIARY
or
INTELLIGENCE SUMMARY.
(Erase heading not required.)

Instructions regarding War Diaries and Intelligence Summaries are contained in F.S. Regs., Part II. and the Staff Manual respectively. Title pages will be prepared in manuscript.

Hour, Date, Place	Summary of Events and Information	Remarks and references to Appendices
10.xi.15 BETHUNE (47)	Fine day. All quiet. Observation impossible 4.30 p.m. to 7 p.m. Wire cutting weekly to begun this week. Ammunition expenditure. Routine orders	1457 1458 1459 1460
11.xi.15	Light frosty sund. Observation impossible 9.15am & 7.15 pm. August. Heavy wire cutting for trench or account of infantry strife. Return of battery positions Ammunition expenditure Routine orders	1461 1462 1463 1464

Army Form C. 2118

WAR DIARY
or
INTELLIGENCE SUMMARY.
(Erase heading not required.)

Instructions regarding War Diaries and Intelligence Summaries are contained in F.S. Regs., Part II. and the Staff Manual respectively. Title pages will be prepared in manuscript.

Hour, Date, Place		Summary of Events and Information	Remarks and references to Appendices
Friday November 12. XI.15 BETHUNE (F)		Wet. Changeable. Light frost. Fair. All quiet. 48th Battery relieved 71st.	1465
		Orders for reliefs	1466
	4 pm	Command of 34th Brigade handed over to 27th Brig.	1467
		Ammunition Expenditure	1468
		Routine orders	
Saturday Friday 13 XI.15		Quiet day. & Communication Expenditure	1469
			1470
		Routine orders	1471
Sunday Saturday 14 XI.15		Observation from Me 10 am to 4 pm. Light fog.	1472
		All quiet	
		Wire cutting to begin	1473
		Ammunition Expenditure	1474
		Command of 64th Bde assumed	

WAR DIARY
or
INTELLIGENCE SUMMARY.
(Erase heading not required.)

Army Form C. 2118

Instructions regarding War Diaries and Intelligence Summaries are contained in F. S. Regs., Part II. and the Staff Manual respectively. Title pages will be prepared in manuscript.

Hour, Date, Place	Summary of Events and Information	Remarks and references to Appendices
Sunday 15.XII.15	Generally quiet, hostile enemy's artillery more active than usual. light snow	1475
	Ammunition expenditure	1476
	Lt Colonel Sandby wounded assumed command on 14th.	
	Lt Gerrard Sanders returned	
Tuesday 16.XII.15	Wet, dull, light hail. All quiet	1477
	Lt General Sanders returned from leave 2 am.	1478
	Ammunition expenditure	1479
	Routine orders	
Wednesday 17.XII.15	Still light fire. All quiet	1480
	Wire cutting proposals	1481
	Routine orders	1482

Army Form C. 2118.

WAR DIARY
or
INTELLIGENCE SUMMARY.
(Erase heading not required.)

Instructions regarding War Diaries and Intelligence Summaries are contained in F.S. Regs., Part II. and the Staff Manual respectively. Title pages will be prepared in manuscript.

Hour, Date, Place	Summary of Events and Information	Remarks and references to Appendices
Thursday 18.XII.15 BETHUNE (47)	Quiet day. Machine gun carried out. Frost at night. Weekly returns for time. Ammunition Expenditure	1783 1784 1785
Friday 19.XII.15	Quiet day, light fair. Further intercepting post (escape). Brief brief. Organization on new front. Ammunition Expenditure Routine orders	1786 1787 1788 1789 1790
Saturday 20.XII.15	Enemy slightly more active than usual. Fair light. Frost at night. Ammunition Expenditure Routine Orders	1491 1492 1493

Army Form C. 2118.

WAR DIARY
or
INTELLIGENCE SUMMARY.
(Erase heading not required.)

Instructions regarding War Diaries and Intelligence Summaries are contained in F.S. Regs., Part II. and the Staff Manual respectively. Title pages will be prepared in manuscript.

Hour, Date, Place	Summary of Events and Information	Remarks and references to Appendices
Sunday 21.XI.15 BETHUNE (17)	Quiet day. No action of importance. Fire light fair.	1794
	Ammunition expenditure	1795
	Routine orders	1796
	15th Divr Artillery to come in a day earlier	1797
Monday 22.XI.15	Very quiet day. Think Bg- no firing by enemy.	1798
	36th Brigade HQ relieves 34th.	1799
	71st Battery relieves 12th Battery 7th Bde.	1800
	70th & 50th Batteries returned to 2nd Divr Command.	1801
	Report on wirecutting tractor	1802
	59th Siege to come under 2nd Divr Com. 23rd.	1803
	Ammunition expenditure	
	Routine orders	
	Map	

WAR DIARY
or
INTELLIGENCE SUMMARY.

Army Form C. 2118.

Hour, Date, Place	Summary of Events and Information	Remarks and references to Appendices
Tuesday 23. XI. 15 BETHUNE (47)	Much fog. Very quiet except for mining activity on which our artillery fired. 71st Brigade relieved 67th. Ammunition expenditure Routine Orders	1504 1505 1506 1507
Wednesday 24. XI. 15	All quiet, but a little mine activity. Weather turned cold. nnn. Ammunition expenditure Routine Orders Command] 71st Bde handed over to 15th Bn. 5 p.m.	1508 1509 1510
Thursday 25. 11.15	Observation possible 8 am to 3.30 pm. Snowy. Exploded a Bosches and Smoke bombing attack on Z. Otherwise quiet. 1 mid A.M. 20 wet. Wrote training instructions Ammunition expenditure Routine Orders	1511 1512 1513 1514

Army Form C. 2118.

WAR DIARY
or
INTELLIGENCE SUMMARY.
(Erase heading not required.)

Instructions regarding War Diaries and Intelligence Summaries are contained in F. S. Regs., Part II. and the Staff Manual respectively. Title pages will be prepared in manuscript.

Hour, Date, Place	Summary of Events and Information	Remarks and references to Appendices
Friday 26.XI.15 BETHUNE (97)	N.W. Wind 13mh. Quiet day. Reaction of importance. Wire cutting begun. Ammunition Expenditure Routine orders	1515 1516 1517 1518
Saturday 27.XI.15	Wind S.E. 5mh. Cold and foggy. All quiet. Some snow. Wire cutting operations continued. Attempt at Bombardment Report on auxiliary means of communication with infantry. Instructions re Crossheads from hostile gun fires. Orders for operations. Ammunition Expenditure. Routine orders	1519 1520 1521 1522 00.8 1523 1524
Sunday 28.XI.15	Wind S.E. 5mh. Cold - Some snow. Bombardment programme carried out. Somewhat delayed by presence of hostile planes. These flew so high that our planes could not reach them. Portions of our Ammunition Expenditure	1525 1526 1527

79
3298

Army Form C. 2118.

WAR DIARY
or
INTELLIGENCE SUMMARY.
(Erase heading not required.)

Instructions regarding War Diaries and Intelligence Summaries are contained in F.S. Regs., Part II. and the Staff Manual respectively. Title pages will be prepared in manuscript.

Hour, Date, Place	Summary of Events and Information	Remarks and references to Appendices
Monday 29.xi.15 BETHUNE	Wind S. Quiet thaw. Some mist.	
	Bombardment continued. Enemy retaliated in May.	1528
	Mine difficult to tell what results were.	1529
	Ammunition Expenditure	1530
	Routine orders	
Tuesday 30.xi.15	Quiet day	1531
	Report on action 28/29	1532
	One gun 7th Ammunition transferred to A Group	1533
	Proposals for renewing operations	1534
	Roll of Officers	1535
	Ammunition Expenditure	1536

DAILY AMMUNITION RETURN.

1st Nov. 15

Piece	Projectile	Code	\multicolumn{10}{c}{BATTERIES}	Total	Per Piece
			50	70	15	48	71	9	16	17	47	56		
18-pr	Guns	48												
	Shrapnel	A	9	13	46	-	37	58	26	15			204	
	H.E.	Ax	-	12	-	-	38	40	-	11			101	
4.5" (Howzr)	Howitzers													
	Shrapnel	B									6		6	
	H.E.	Bx									-			

DAILY DIARY

Z group.   1-11-15.

9th Batt. fired on working party in trench running N. of DIAMOND DOOR COTTAGE They ceased work. 9:30am. 11 am 1:30 pm 3:30 pm shelled ETNA.

15th Batt. fired three times on Minenwerfer and last night at 6 am on support trenches behind MINE point.

17th Batt. searched around LES BRIQUES haystacks and fired on german trenches & both in retaliation. Registered LEAN-TO (LEAF) COTTAGE

9th How Batt. fired on RYANS keep and A21d7.1 to stop Minenwerfer.

71st Batt. fired on MINE point support trenches during the night; and three times to-day in retaliation.

71st Batt. and 15th Batt. fired on support trenches behind Mine point last night at request of infantry, at a slow rate to keep the germans down while work was done on saps etc.

"A" Form.
Army Form C. 2121.

MESSAGES AND SIGNALS.

| TO | R.A. 2nd Division |

Sender's Number.	Day of Month.	In reply to Number	AAA
OK/59	1st		

Daily Report 34th Bde.

50th Bty — Very quiet on 50th Bty front all day, except when enemy retaliated to bombarding of SINGLE TREE by H.A.R.

70th Bty — fired at 9.20 am & 9.35 am on houses & road in A.17.c and on AUCHY-HAISNES road in retaliation to pip-squeaks on CAMBRIN & main road

56th Bty — Nil

Observation impossible from 4.40 pm to 7.15 am. Light very indifferent all day.

A.T. Sloan
a/Adj. 34th Bde

HOSTILE shelling took place on Cambrin
cross roads and second line trenches
His fire on our second line trenches
does not appear to be observed
He also shelled 6th Bde Hqrs (2 cas) and
Tunnelling Coys house all 77 mm.
He shelled Vermelles + roads and
Vermelles — Sailly Labourse road with
105 mm. also Annequin church 105mm
RETALIATION The Germans required
retaliation in twelve instances
by 15th 17th 21st + 47th Batts.
WORK Work is reported in trench
N of Diamond door cottage A22d88
The Germans are sapping out to
ETNA on E. a quantity of periscopes
and some new work were removed
by our shelling
9th Batt leave two guns in
old position to shoot on ETNA etc
A white triangular sign was observed
A23c1.1 or A22d8.4 place not identified.
Light poor

Rodd M.
Adj. 411th Bde.

2nd Division Artillery Orders

by

Brigadier-General G.H.SANDERS, D.S.O., Comdg. R.A., 2nd Divn.

1st November, 1915.

1079. R.A. ORDERS.

Were not issued yesterday, 31-10-1915.

1080. LEAVE.

The new allotment of leave is as follows:-

	Officers.	Men.	
Tuesday.	1	-	41st Brigade.
	1	-	44th "
	-	27.	41st "
	-	14.	34th "
	-	9.	44th "
	-	6.	D.A.C.
Wednesday.	1.	-	D.A.C.
	-	56.	34th Brigade.
	-	1.	D.A.C. (with C.O.)
Thursday.	2.	-	34th Brigade.
	-	56.	36th "
Friday.	2.	-	36th Brigade.
	-	56.	41st "
Saturday.	2.	-	41st Brigade.
	-	56.	44th "
Sunday.	2.	-	44th Brigade.
	-	56.	D.A.C.
Monday.	1.	-	D.A.C.
	-	34.	36th Brigade.
	-	9.	7th Mountain Bty.
	-	2.	Armoured Cars.
	-	7.	41st Brigade.
	-	3.	D.A.C.
	-	2.	Spare.

This allotment is liable to temporary reduction. In that event the unit with greatest number going will be notified of the amount of the reduction. O's C. Brigades will report on Sundays at 8 p.m. the number of men who have been out throughout the war who have not had leave. Sunday's allotment is not to be included in this return.

Leave will now be given for 10 days, counting from time of leaving BETHUNE at midnight to time of leaving LONDON to catch 7 p.m. boat from SOUTHAMPTON on the 10th day.

Train leaves BETHUNE at midnight, all men should carry one day's rations.

L.G. BUXTON Captain R.A.

Staff Captain R.A. 2nd Division.

"A" Form.
Army Form C. 2121.

MESSAGES AND SIGNALS.

Prefix	Code	Words	Charge	This message is on a/c of:	Rec'd. at ___ m.
Office of Origin and Service Instructions.					Date
		Sent At ___ m.		Service.	From
		To			
		By		(Signature of "Franking Officer.")	By

TO R.A. 2nd Division

| Sender's Number. | Day of Month. | In reply to Number | AAA |
| OK/61 | 2nd | | |

Daily Report 34th Bde

50th Bty — Report that house behind triangle at about A.17.c.7.2 has had the roof propped up and a window opened. This house has always been suspected as an O.P. and PONT FIXE was shelled in the afternoon.

70th Bty — Fired at 7.45 pm, 1.10 pm & 1.20 pm on AUCHY and HAISNES in retaliation to pipsqueaks on CAMBRIN and main road.

56th Bty — Nil

Observation impossible between 4.30 pm and 6.30 am. Light fairly good all day aaa North Wind

From
Place
Time

The above may be forwarded as now corrected. (Z)

A.T. Sloan
Lieut
a/Adj 54th Bde

DAILY DIARY

Z group.   2-11-15

9th Batt. fired on ETNA and on sap
N of Etna at irregular intervals
during the night.
15th Batt. fired on Auchy in retaliation
17th Batt. nothing to report
47th Batt.   "
71st Batt. fired on Auchy in retaliation.

Observation bad light indifferent
Germans shelled Cambrin + xroads

"Queens" and 1/4/1 relieved by Oxon Bucks
and Worcesters. Communication with
batteries and regiments established.

F. Todd lt.
Adj Z group.

DAILY AMMUNITION RETURN.

2.XI.15

Piece	Projectile	Code	\[Batteries\] 30	70	15	48	71	9	16	17	47	56			Total	Per Piece
18-pr	Guns		6	6	6	6	6	6	6	6	—	—				
	Shrapnel	A	12	8	—	—	—	28	34	10						92
	H. E.	Ax			16	—	25	36	—	—						77
4.5" (Howzr)	Howitzers															
	Shrapnel	A								—	13					13
	H. E.	Bx								12	—					12

1429

2nd Division Artillery Orders

by

Brigadier-General G.H.SANDERS, D.S.O., Comdg. R.A., 2nd Divn.

2nd November, 1915.

1081. LEAVE.

Leave has now been reduced to 50 per day. Allotment therefore is as follows:-

Officers - same.
ON 3rd, 4th, 5th, 6th, 7th. - 48 men instead of 56.

8th	31 men	-	36th Brigade.
	9 "	-	7th Mountain Bty.
	1 "	-	Armoured Cars.
	5 "	-	41st Brigade.
	2 "	-	Spare.
9th.	26 men.	-	41st Brigade.
	10 "	-	34th "
	6 "	-	44th "
	6 "	-	D.A.C.

1082. RECREATION ROOM.

It has been arranged that the 2nd Division Recreation Room, RUE d'AIRE, shall be open from 8 p.m. to 11 p.m. each evening for the use of men of 2nd Divn. proceeding on leave by the midnight train. No one else will be admitted.

1083. CLOTHES BRUSHES.

Clothes Brushes will be maintained by Units at the following scale :-

10 per Battery.

Indents for first issue and to replace unserviceable brushes will be submitted to D.A.D.O.S. (Authority 2nd Divn. Q. 3773, 1st Novr.).

L.G.BUXTON. Capt, R.A.,
Staff Captain, R.A., 2nd Divn.

- AFTER ORDERS -

1084. REFILLING.

Hour of re-filling from to-morrow inclusive will be 9-0 a.m.

"A" Form.
MESSAGES AND SIGNALS.

Army Form C. 2121.

TO	R A 2nd Division

Sender's Number.	Day of Month	In reply to Number	
OK/66	3rd		AAA

Daily Report 34th Bde

50th Bty fired at suspected machine gun emplacement at A16c 3.5 at 11.15 am aaa dispersed working party at CULVERT at 4.30pm aaa. Quiet day.

70th Bty At 9.55 am fired on Germans seen in front line trenches & behind trucks at A16c 8.5. At 10.30 am at front line again Slue movement was seen at A21 c 8.8 aaa fired at front line again at 1.30 pm & 1.50 pm.

56th Bty fired shrapnel at stopping party working at A16a 4.4 aaa at 2.20 pm & at 2.40 pm dispersed working party at A16a 5.3

From
Place Observation impossible between 4.30pm
Time and 7 am. Light good.

"A" Form.
MESSAGES AND SIGNALS.
Army Form C. 2121.

TO	R.A. 2nd Dv.	

Sender's Number.	Day of Month	In reply to Number	
* OK/66	3w.		AAA

Information. This morning Germans came out in places from their trenches and stood on the ground behind making signs and shouting. Our Infantry thought they might be intending to surrender, as small white flags or handkerchiefs were waved in 2 or 3 places, but they showed no signs of doing so + at about 10am got into their trenches again aaa 70th Bty did not fire at them as our own infantry were shewing themselves + the O.C. Bn asked 70th not to shoot in case they wished to surrender aaa About 70 or 100 shewed themselves between brickstacks + the road

A.T. Sloan Lieut
a/Adjt 34th Bde

DAILY DIARY.

Z group.   3-11-15.

9th Batt. shelled house in AUCHY A22 d 8.4 where movement of Germans was noticed. Fired on working party near LONE FARM the party put up three white flags. Fired on traffic on Road A24 B 05 at 2 pm. These parties were dispersed. Another party stopped work in CHATEAU ALLEY when 9th Batt fired.

Guns were registered on ETNA from rear position.

15th Batt. nothing to report.

17th Batt. fired on german trenches at 10.15 am. retaliated on trenches for Trench mortar bombing.

71st Batt fired on german trenches by request.

47th How Batt nothing to report

HOSTILE SHELLING. Germans fired on our trenches with 105 mm & 77 mm. They also fired on La Bassée road and vicinity of Barrier and Cambrin church with 77mm.

WORK. There is a small gap in enemy wire at A.21.d.6.4. More work seems to have been done on trenches in A.28 central comm. trenches into MADAGASCAR trench having been dug. Other working parties as reported.

- at 10.35 am HERTS reported some of enemy standing on parapet N of road waving a white flag!!
- at 10.40 am WORCESTERS reported germans manning 2nd line trench with fixed bayonets, no movement was however seen from O.B!

Light quite fair.

Rodd sh.
Adj. 41st Bde

MESSAGES AND SIGNALS.

Army Form C. 2121.

TO	R.A 2 Dw

Sender's Number	Day of Month	In reply to Number	
	3.		AAA

HERTS report GERMANS are standing on their parapet just North of LA BASSEE Road waving white handkerchiefs

From: H1 Bde
Time: 10.40 am

"A" Form. Army Form C. 2121.

MESSAGES AND SIGNALS.

Prefix	Code	m.	Words	Charge	This message is on a/c of:	Recd. at	m.
Office of Origin and Service Instructions.			Sent At___m. To___ By___		___Service. (Signature of "Franking Officer")	Date___ From___ By___	

TO		R.A. 2 Div	

Sender's Number	Day of Month	In reply to Number	AAA
	3.		

Last report Germans are lining their 2nd line Trenches with fixed Bayonets

From
Place: Z Group.
Time

The above may be forwarded as now corrected. (Z)

Censor. Signature of Addressor or person authorised to telegraph in his name

* This line should be erased if not required.

MESSAGES AND SIGNALS.

Army Form C. 2121.
No. of Message 67

Prefix	Code	m.	Words	Charge
Office of Origin and Service Instructions			Sent At m. To By	*This message is on a/c of:* Service. (Signature of "Franking Officer")

Recd. at .... m.
Date ....
From ....
By ....

TO ~~RA 5 Bde~~
~~5 Bde~~

Sender's Number: 9430
Day of Month: 3
In reply to Number:
AAA

Fire is to be opened at once on all occasions when enemy exposes himself and offers a suitable target aaa fire is to be opened at once now on both first and second lines where Germans are seen assembling aaa Addressed RA 5th Bde 6th Bde

(Print)

From 2 Div.
Place
Time 11.15 am.

Davidson Capt

"A" Form.
MESSAGES AND SIGNALS.

Army Form C. 2121.

Prefix	Code	m.	Words	Charge	This message is on a/c of	Recd. at	m.
Office of Origin and Service Instructions.			Sent		Service.	Date	
			At ___ m.			From	
			To		(Signature of "Franking Officer.")	By	
			By				

TO   3 / 41 Bde / Bde ~~crossed out~~

Sender's Number: Hou Shot   Day of Month: In reply to Number: AAA

Fire is to be opened at once when enemy exposes himself and offers a visible target

From: R A 71 Div
Place:
Time: 11:50 am

"A" Form.
Army Form C. 2121.
MESSAGES AND SIGNALS.

TO: RA Q

Sender's Number: GA 81
Day of Month: 3
AAA

Following from RA 1st Corps begins one section 7th mountain battery is placed under the orders of the 2nd Div with effect from 4.11.15 aaa section commander to report to Hd Qrs 34th Bde RFA at 10 am tomorrow aaa ends aaa does this arrangement suit you aaa addressed RA 2nd Div repeated Q

From: 2nd Div
Time: 11 pm

1433

DAILY AMMUNITION RETURN.

3.XI.15

Piece	Projectile	Code	50	70	15	48	71	9	16	17	47	56			Total	Per Piece
18-pr Guns																
	Shrapnel	A	–	35	22	–	29	70	35	79					270	
	H.E.	Ax	–	19	11	–	–	52	–	1					83	
4.5" (Howzr)	Howitzers																
	Shrapnel	Z													–	
	H.E.	Bx													–	

2nd Division Artillery Orders

by

Brigadier-General G.H.SANDERS, D.S.O., Comdg.R.A., 2nd Divn.

3rd November, 1915.

1085. LEAVE - OFFICER'S.

Officers proceeding on leave can, if they wish, go by the train leaving MERVILLE at 4-15 a.m. There is a clean-looking Estaminet quite close to Merville Station. Officers going this way should return the same way. The train leaves Victoria at 1-15 p.m. and arrives Merville about 2 a.m.

Officers should arrange for their horses to meet them at Merville.

L.G.BUXTON, Capt, R.A.,
Staff Captain, R.A., 2nd Division.

R.A. 2nd Div.

Positions

Battery	Ref. 1/40000 Map
34th Bde —	
50	F 18 a 3.2
70	F 24 c 9.2
41st Bde	
9	F 18 c 3.1
17	F 24 c 5.8
71 (4 guns)	F 24 c 8.4
15 (4 guns)	G 8 a 0.5
44th Bde 47th	F 30 c 7.3
~~BAC~~ 56th	A 20 a 5.1
B.A.C. 34	E 10 b 6.2
36	E 5 d 10.1
41	E 10 b 7.1
44	Champ de Mars Bethune Rue Gambetta
7th Mountain Section	will go into action about G 2 b

Ra 2 Div
9.11.15

J M Murray Major
Bde R A

"A" Form.
MESSAGES AND SIGNALS.

Army Form C. 2121.

TO: R.A. 2nd Division

Sender's Number: OR/72
Day of Month: 4th

AAA

Daily Report 34th Bde

50th Bty fired at party of Germans reported to be working on the South TOW PATH by the Infantry at 8.45 am. aaa fired at another working party S.E. of the N.E. BRICKSTACK in afternoon. At 4.30 pm enemy blew up a mine in front of JERUSALEM HILL doing considerable damage to our trenches

70th Bty fired on AUCHY–HAISNES Road at 5pm in retaliation to pipsqueaks on HARLEY STREET.

56th Bty. At 10.16 pm last night fired in retaliation to MINENWERFER active

"A" Form.
MESSAGES AND SIGNALS.
Army Form C. 2121.

Prefix	Code	m.	Words	Charge	This message is on a/c of:	Recd. at	m.
Office of Origin and Service Instructions.			Sent			Date	
			At	m.	Service.	From	
			To				
			By		(Signature of "Franking Officer.")	By	

| TO | | R.A. 2nd Div | | |

| Sender's Number. | Day of Month | In reply to Number | | AAA |
| OK/72 | 4th | | | |

on the main road and dispersed a working party at A16 a 4.4

Observation impossible between 4.40 pm and 12 noon.

Information 50th Bty report German was seen to come out between 3rd & 4th trucks from rt hand end of rear train & get into trench there.

PONTEFIXE was intermittently shelled throughout the night & also for a short time this afternoon

No further signs of Germans shewing themselves between row & mid stacks

A. Sloan
a/Adj 34th Bde

From				
Place				
Time				

The above may be forwarded as now corrected. (Z)

Censor. Signature of Addressor or person authorised to telegraph in his name.

* This line should be erased if not required.
(774-5) —McC. & Co. Ltd., London.— W 1789/1402. 150,000. 8/15. Forms C 2121/10.

DAILY DIARY

4.10.15

Z Group.

5th Batt. Nothing to report.

9th Batt. Registered a section of various points

17th Batt. Fired on German Sniping Post, also on AUCHY and PEKIN TRENCH.

71st Batt. Fired on Trench running NORTH from THREE CABERETS, and on house about A 23 c 9 3, on which 15 direct hits were obtained without doing any damage. This house must be fortified.

47th Batt. Nothing to report.

HOSTILE SHELLING.
Germans fired on VERMELLES CROSS ROADS. 5 rounds 77 mm from direction of AUCHY, and 4 rounds 105 mm from DOUVRIN

WORK. No fresh work observed.

— Thick mist untill Midday, afternoon light fair.

— 3 Germans, apparently 2 officers and 1 man, carrying Map case and drawing board, were seen to walk from THREE CABERETS towards the CEMETERY, their destination was obscured by LES BRIQUES.

L.D. Reeves. 2/Lt.
a/adj 41st Bde

DAILY AMMUNITION RETURN.

4.XI.15

Piece	Projectile	Code	\<BATTERIES\> 30	70	15	48	71	9	16	17	47	56			Total	Per Piece
18-pr Guns																
	Shrapnel	A	28	24	-	-	3	4	45	5					119	
	H.E.	Ax	12	17	-	-	-	30	-	-					59	
4.5" (Howzr)	Howitzers																
	Shrapnel	X								-	16				16	
	H.E.	Bx								-	11				11	

2nd Division Artillery Orders

by

Lieut.-Colonel C.R.P.PARRY, Comdg.R.A., 2nd Division.

4th November, 1915.

1086. POSTING.

Captain R. FERNIE is transferred from D.A.C., to command 41st B.A.C., Vice ROBERTSON sick, with effect from 1st November,

1087. LEAVE.

Men going on leave are not allowed to enter the Station before 11-0 p.m. The Divisional Recreation Room, Rue d'Aire, is open until 11-0 p.m., and men should wait there.

1088. TRENCHES - TELEPHONE WIRES.

The C.R.E., will tomorrow fill in the trenches as detailed in 2nd Divn. R.A., O.20 of the 30th October.

The Dogs-legs therein mentioned are now complete.

L.G.BUXTON, Capt, R.A.

Staff Captain, R.A., 2nd Divn.

DAILY DIARY.

5.11.15

Z Group.

9th Batt. Registered two guns on DIAMOND DOOR Cottage.
Fired on enemy trenches in retaliation.
Registered two guns on house A.8, B78, were small parties of about 6 Germans were seen passing through gate.
3.45pm fired on ETNA at request of Infantry.

16th Batt Fired on minenwerfer at MINE POINT, checked some registrations

17th Batt Fired on German Observation Post, also on a party moving on the right of AUCHY.
Fired on observers in front trench and some Germans exposing themselves.

47th Batt Nothing to report.

71st Batt. Fired on a likely observation post in AUCHY, also on minenwerfer at MINE POINT.

WORK.
From RAILWAY COTTAGE A.28.6.4505
to A.28.b.2.3. Fresh enemy wire
was observed, where it crosses the
Railway track, also fresh earth
appears to have been thrown up.

HOSTILE SHELLING.
Enemy shelled VERMELLES CROSS
ROADS at 10.30 am, from the direction
of AUCHY.
Enemy also shelled our trenches with
30 rounds of 77 mm opposite MINE
POINT.

It was impossible to observe this
morning untill noon when mist
began to rise. Light in the early
afternoon was good.

J.R. Reeves. 2/Lt R.F.A.
a/adj 41st Bde.

"A" Form.
MESSAGES AND SIGNALS.
Army Form C. 2121.

Prefix	Code	m.	Words	Charge	This message is on a/c of:	Recd. at	m.
Office of Origin and Service Instructions.			Sent			Date	
			At	m.	Service.	From	
			To				
			By		(Signature of "Franking Officer.")	By	

TO: R.A. 2nd Division

Sender's Number.	Day of Month	In reply to Number	AAA
* OK/75	5th		

	Daily Report 34th Bde		
12 Bty	Enemy working on trench S of N.E Brickstack and fired at SINGLE TRUCK		
70th Bty	At 10.25am fired on working party at A 21 a 8.7 in front line trench. The first round of H.E fell in the middle of them. At 11am & 1.45pm fired in retaliation & at 2.20pm at horse A 22 a 8.7 from which columns of smoke were seen. At 3.55 pm on working party putting up sandbags at A 21 a 87		
56 Bty	At 11.5 am fired on trench W of TRIANGLE & barges in CANAL DOCK in retaliation to shelling of CUINCHY. 1.58 p.m fired on working party at A.16.d.17. 2.55 pm fired on working party at A 16 a 5.6 Observation impossible 4.30pm — 9am.		

From
Place
Time

Wind N.N.W. (Z)

J. Lewis 2nd Lieut
34th Bde

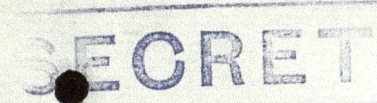

R.A. 2nd Division.	No.1 Group, H.A.R.)
R.A. 7th Division.	No.4 Group, H.A.R.)
R.A.12th Division.	2nd Division.) For
7th Brigade, R.G.A.	7th Division.) information.
No. 5 Group, H.A.R..	12th Division.)
	1st Corps.)

No. 1/R.A.S./105-9.   2nd Nov.1915.

1. The Corps Commander wishes special efforts made to locate hostile guns situated within 2000 yards of our Trenches.

2. After such a gun or guns have been accurately located, directly they re-open fire the Divisional Artillery Commander in whose area the target is situated will arrange to engage it on the following plan:-

   Every gun and howitzer under his command whose arc of fire permits, will fire for two minutes with H.E.
   The Divisional Artillery Commander will further arrange with No. 5 Group, H.A.R., 7th Brigade, R.G.A., and the neighbouring divisional Artillery to turn on as much fire as they can at the same moment.
   The 60-Pdr Batteries should also be asked ~~to co-operate.~~

   2nd Divisional Artillery
   No. B.M. Inst/36
   Date

   S.W.H. Rawlins
   Major, R.A.,
   Staff Officer, R.A., 1st Corps.

Z group
A group
36th Brigade
7th Brigade
ELLERSHAWS BRIGADE } For information

No 5 Group H.A.R
7th Brigade R.G.A.
2nd Div. G.S.

In order to carry this into effect the following procedure will be followed by field artillery brigades.

As soon as a hostile gun within the zone opens, the brigade to whom it is reported will inform the other brigade and also ELLERSHAWS Brigade, No 5 Group HAR, and 7th Brigade RGA naming a time about 1/4 hour ahead at which hos batteries will open fire.

ELLERSHAWS Brigade, No 5 Group and 7th Brigade

have undertaken to inform field artillery brigades in the same way. They are all connected with 2nd Division telephone exchange.

2. The hostile guns at present located within our zone and within 2000 yards of our trenches are –

    A 17 d central
    A 18 c 0.8
    A 23 a 6.6
    A 23 b 8.2 to 8.5
    A 29 a 3.5
    A 22 d 8.4
    A 23 c 5.7
    A 23 d 1.9
    A 23 d 7.7
    A 29 b 1.6

3. Corrections and additions to this list should be reported to this office, and will be further circulated from time to time.

4. Experience will show whether the notice of the hour is sufficient.

R.A. 2 Div.
5. 11. 15

DAILY AMMUNITION RETURN.

5. XI. 15

Piece	Projectile	Code	%C	70	15	48	71	9	16	17	47	56		Total	Per Piece
18-pr Guns															
	Shrapnel	A	12	1	14	–	9	81	16	45				178	
	H.E.	AH	11		14	–	–	25	29	–	22			101	
4.5" Howitzers (Howzr)															
	Shrapnel	X							–	16					
	H.E.	BX							–	6					

2nd Division Artillery Orders

by

Lieut.-Colonel, C.E.P.PARRY, Comdg.R.A., 2nd Division.

5th November, 1915.

1089. DENTIST.

Reference R.A.Order No.373, dated 18-8-1915.

The Dentist will not attend at SEMINAIRE ST. VAAST until further orders.

1090. CHILLED FEET & FROSTBITE - PREVENTION OF.

Reference G.R.O., No. 1229, dated 29-10-1915.

O's C.Units should report whether they require basins for washing feet, in addition to those to be issued for ablution rooms.

1091 Telephone Equipment.

It is notified for information that any small insulators required by R.A.Units should be obtained from the Signal Officer of the formation to which they are attached.

(1st Army O.S.30/68 3-11-15. 2nd Dn.Q.3801- R.A.490.)

L.G.BUXTON.Capt, R.A.,
Staff Captain, R.A., 2nd Divn.

DAILY DIARY.

6.11.15.

Z. Group.

9ᵗʰ Batt. Fired on a small working party at Les BRIQUES, also on enemy gun A 23 C 5.7.

15ᵗʰ Batt. Fired on Support Trenches, FRANKS KEEP - POPE'S NOSE also Les BRIQUES 10th in retaliation. Fired on Minenwerfer at MINE POINT.

17ᵗʰ Batt. Twice fired in retaliation to Trench Mortars at the request of the infantry. Fired in retaliation to 4.2 shrapnel on our front trench

47ᵗʰ Batt. Nothing to report.

71ˢᵗ Batt. Fired on AUCHY during the morning, at 3pm on a Minenwerfer about A 21 d 7.1. also on MINE POINT and RAILWAY TRENCH in retaliation.

Hostile Shelling.

Enemy shelled our front trenches also reserve trenches near MAISON

ROUGE, later VERMELLES CROSS ROADS.

This evening enemy shelled LA BASSEE ROAD with field guns and heavy, from the direction of LA BASSEE.

Work. No enemy work was observed to day, as the light was very bad. Observation has been impossible all day

R. Reeves 2/L
q adj 41 Bde RFA

"A" Form.
Army Form C. 2121.
MESSAGES AND SIGNALS.

No. of Message _____

Prefix	Code	m.	Words	Charge	This message is on a/c of:	Recd. at _____ m.
Office of Origin and Service Instructions.			Sent			Date _____
			At _____ m.		_____ Service.	From _____
			To			
			By		(Signature of "Franking Officer.")	By

TO		R.A. 2nd Div.		

Sender's Number.	Day of Month	In reply to Number		AAA
* AK/80	6th			

50th Bty. Did not fire

70th Bty. 11. am fired on working party about A 21 b 83. They were seen by the infantry in the mist, + reported by them to 70th Bty
3. pm fired on ROAD A 16 d 82 in retaliation for shelling of HARLEY ST

56th Bty. 10.40 pm fired at MINENWERFER at request of HERTS.

Observation impossible 4.45 pm — 7.20 am After 8. am it has not been possible to see the trenches all day. About 3 pm this afternoon the enemy dropped about six PIPSQUEAKS in vicinity of CAMBRIN CHURCH

From
Place
Time

The above may be forwarded as now corrected. (Z)

J.W. Lewis 2nd Lieut

Censor. Signature of Addressor or person authorised to telegraph in his name.

34th Bde

DAILY AMMUNITION RETURN.

6.XI.15

Piece	Projectile	Code	\multicolumn{11}{c	}{BATTERIES}	Total	Per Piece
			30	70	15	48	71	9	16	17	47	56		
18-pr Guns														
	Shrapnel	A	6	14	44	–	51	62	32	53			262	
	H. E.	Ax	2	20	–	–	22	27	–	34			105	
4.5" (Howzr) Howitzers														
	Shrapnel	B							–				–	
	H. E.	Bx							–				–	

2nd Division Artillery Orders

by

Lieut.-Colonel C.R.P.PARRY, Comdg.R.A., 2nd Division.

6th November, 1915.

1092. DIVINE SERVICE.

Divine Service for all units in BETHUNE will be held at the Chapel, RUE d'AIRE, at 10-30 a.m to-morrow.

Divine Service for all batteries in action will be held at TOURBIERES loop crossed roads at 2-30 p.m.

L.G.BUXTON, Capt, R.A.,

Staff Captain, R.A., 2nd Divn.

- NOTICES. -

LOST. -   On the night of the 3rd Novr. 1915, two horses. Both about 15.2, and branded on Hind Quarters. Colour Blue Roan and Strawberry Roan respectively. Any information should be sent to H.Q., 36th Brigade R.F.A.

LOST -   About 10-30 a.m. yesterday - a Mule - Description Dark Brown Mare.   Marks as under:-
"H" cut in hair on near side of neck.
3/2 D.A.C., Branded on off fore.
No.90, Branded on near fore.
Information concerning same should be forwarded to O.C., 2nd Division Ammunition Column.

DAILY DIARY.

7.11.16

Z Group.

9th Batt. Fired on enemy trenches in retaliation to hostile bombing. Fired on and dispersed working party in A 22 d 9 6.

17th Batt. Fired in retaliation to Minenwerfer also in retaliation to Germans shelling our front line with 77mm. In the afternoon fired on Snipers Post later in retaliation again.

15th Batt. Fired in retaliation several times during the day, twice on Minen-werfer. Fired on likely observation Post A 23 a 1 4.

47th Batt. Nothing to report, except fired on MINE POINT at point 97 in retaliation

71st Batt. Fired several rounds of HE and shrapnel into AUCHY, and twice on Minenwerfer at MINE POINT.

HOSTILE SHELLING. Enemy shelled

our front line trenches this morning with 77 mm and 4·2. Later SIMS KEEP and opposite MINE POINT with 105 m Howi. from the direction of VIOLANES.

WORK. Enemy have thrown up more earth from RAILWAY COTTAGE to A 28 b 28, and fresh wire from this point in an Easterly direction to about A 28 b 3·5 3·5.

— No observation was possible during the morning owing to the mist, which rose a little later. Light was very poor all day.

Reeves 2/r
9 adj 41st Bde RFA.

"A" Form, MESSAGES AND SIGNALS.

Army Form C. 2121.

TO R.A. 2nd Division

Sender's Number.	Day of Month	In reply to Number	AAA
OK/85	7th		

Daily Report 34th Bde.

50th Bty — fired on N.E. Brickstack at 11.15 am in reply to MINENWERFER aaa

70th Bty — At 7 pm & 9.50 pm fired on AUCHY-HAISNES Road & front line trenches respectively, in reply to shelling of main road aaa. At 8.15 pm & 11.20 am retaliated to pip-squeaks aaa

56th Bty — At 8 pm fired behind BRICKSTACKS in reply to howitzer fire near main road aaa. At 11.35 am fired at trenches aaa behind BRICKSTACKS in retaliation to MINENWERFER. At 2.4 pm dispersed working party at A.1.c.6.3

From Place: Observation posts between
Time: 11.30 am & 4.20 pm

2nd Division Artillery Observing Stations

Area	Station	Loop hole	No of Observrs	Occupant
Z	WILSONS HO.		1	9th ✓
	CURRAGH GRANGE	1	1	47th Battery ✓
		2	1	62 Bde
		3	1	62 Bde
	FOUR HUNDRED	1	1	15th Battery ✓
		2	2	71st Battery ✓
				33rd Heavy
A	THE RUIN		2	
	TOWER OF BABEL	1	2	47th Battery ✓
				56th "
		2	2	81st Siege
				10th Siege
				5th Siege
	BRADDELL CASTLE	1	1	17th Battery ✓
		2	2	70th Battery ✓
	MOUNTAIN HO.	1	1	70th Battery (alt.) ✓
		2	2	56th Battery
		3	1	Mountain Artillery ✓
	KINGSCLERE	2	1	81st Siege (alt.)
		1	1	HAR
				56th Battery (alt.) ✓
	HUNVIEW	1	1	56th Battery ✓
		2	1	81st Siege
		3	2	50th Battery ✓
	" ANNEXE	1	1	HAR
		2	1	50th Battery (alt.) ✓
	BRADDELL CASTLE	3	1	70th Battery
		4	2	56th alt. ✓

Above are Stations in use. List of others will follow.

Murray
Major

7.11.15

DAILY AMMUNITION RETURN.

7.XI.15

Piece	Projectile	Code	\multicolumn{10}{c	}{BATTERIES}	Total	Per Piece
			5C	70	15	48	71	9	16	17	47	56		
18-pr	Guns													
	Shrapnel	A	53	-	82	-	82	33	12	72	-	-	309	
	H.E.	Ax	15	-	6	-	127	9	-	-	-	-	257	
4.5" (owzr)	Howitzers													
	Shrapnel	Z								-	-		-	
	H.E.	Bx								-	3		3	

1450

2nd Division Artillery Orders

by

Lieut.-Colonel C.R.P.PARRY, Comdg.R.A., 2nd Division.

7th November, 1915.

1093 LEAVE.

Leave has been reduced to 30 men per day. Officers as before. New allotment as follows :-

Monday.	-	15 men	-	36th Brigade.
		9 "	-	7th Mountain Battery.
		1 "	-	Armoured Cars.
		3 "	-	D.A.C.
		1 "	-	Spare.
Tuesday.	-	15 men	-	41st Brigade.
		7 "	-	34th "
		5 "	-	44th "
		1 "	-	D.A.C.
Wednesday.	-	28 men	-	34th Brigade.
Thursday.	-	28 men	-	36th "
Friday.	-	28 men	-	41st "
Saturday.	-	28 men	-	44th "
Sunday.	-	28 men	-	D.A.C.

1094. ABSENTEES.

O's.C.Units should report at once to A.P.M., the names of any N.C.O's or men who have been absent for more than five days, who have not been accounted for.

1095. LEAVE (again).

From to-night inclusive all N.C.O's and men going on leave will parade at 10-45 p.m. under the leave conducting officer in the GRANDE PLACE, BETHUNE facing the clock in the same order as heretofore.

L.G.BUXTON, Capt, R.A.,
Staff Captain, R.A., 2nd Divn.

DAILY DIARY.

8.11.15

Z. Group.

9th Batt. Fired on ETNA in retaliation to bombing, shelled just south of LA BASSEE ROAD on a minenwerfer, also on 2nd line enemy trench 50 yds North of Point E.
A working party was observed in A22d96 and was dispersed. Retaliated several times in the afternoon.

15th Batt. Retaliated on Minenwerfer at MINE POINT. Checked registrations, and fired later on POPES NOSE and MINE POINT both in retaliation.

17th Batt. Fired on minenwerfer in retaliation on German new work A21 d 66 also in A22 d 22.

47th Batt. Fired on RYANS KEEP several times in retaliation also on some Germans seen in A22 d 88.

71st Fired into AUCHY with HE and shrapnel also on RAILWAY TRENCH in retaliation.

HOSTILE SHELLING.
Enemy to day shelled our front line
line & communication trenches in the
morning, also the path from CAMBRIN
CHURCH to MAISON ROUGE.
A minenwerfer was rather active just
south of the LA BASSEE ROAD, shells
bursting in BRICKSTACKS.

D. Reeves 2/Lt
a/adj 41st Bde

"A" Form.
Army Form C. 2121.
MESSAGES AND SIGNALS.

TO: RA 2nd Divn

Sender's Number: OK/91
Day of Month: 8th
AAA

Daily Report 34th Bde [A Group]

10th Bty. Located & registered battery of field guns (by flashes) at A.11.d.7.4. This battery was first observed on the 5th but owing to mist could not be located.
Fired several times in retaliation for minenwerfer (not located) & pip-squeaks. The latter became active after 2 p.m.

70th Bty. Fired at 3.45 p.m. on 1st & 2nd line trenches in retaliation for 4.2" How. shelling on A.1.

56th Bty. (How.) Fired in retaliation to minenwerfer at 11.35 am. which fired on A.2.
Fired at working party at A.16.a.6.4. three times during the day.

7th Mountain. Registered brickstacks F.G.H. and N.E. brickstack.

"A" Form. Army Form C. 2121.
MESSAGES AND SIGNALS.

TO — RA 2nd Divn.

Sender's Number: OK/91. Day of Month: 8th. AAA

7th Mountain Bty. — Also registered the CULVERT A.16.c.4.7.

Observation impossible between 4.45 pm and 7.15 am.

At 8.15 am, enemy lit a large fire behind N.E. Brickstack.

A Durand /.
Adj. 34th Bde.

DAILY AMMUNITION RETURN.

8.XI.15

Piece	Projectile	Code	BATTERIES										Total	Per Piece
			50	70	15	48	71	9	16	17	47	56		
18-pr Guns														
	Shrapnel	A	82	-	19	-	30	126	37	46			340	
	H.E.	Ax	5	-	73	-	59	27	-	23			187	
4.5" (Howzr)	Howitzers													
	Shrapnel	Z									18		18	
	H.E.	Bx							32	82			114	

2nd Division Artillery Orders

by

Lieut.-Colonel C.R.P.PARRY, Comdg.R.A., 2nd Division.

8th November,1915.

1096. CURRY COMBS.

It has been decided that Curry Combs are not to be issued on active service.

1097. LATRINE BUCKETS.

Latrine Buckets are now available for distribution. Apply A.D.M.S., stating numbers of men in unit.

L.G.BUXTON, Capt, R.A.

Staff Captain, R.A., 2nd Divn

DAILY DIARY.

Z Group.   9.11.15.

9th Batt. Dispersed a working Party in B19
  c 33, also fired on a party walking
  Westwards from house B19 A 04.
  Fired on AUCHY in retaliation.
15th Batt. Shelled a likely O.P. in AUCHY
  about A 23 c 44, also LONE FARM.
  Fired on another O.P. in AUCHY A 23 a 1.5
17th Batt. Fired on working party and new
  work at A 29 a 55. Retaliated on German trenches. at the request of Infantry fired on Sniping Post
47th Batt. Fired on minenwerfer in RYANS
  KEEP. several occasions in retaliation
71st Batt. Fired on working party A 22 d 19
  also on 3 Germans felling a tree about
  A 30 c 94. Shelled AUCHY several
  times in retaliation.
  Inspected 2 houses in AUCHY
  O.P. A 23 a 23 and A 30 d
  fired on both.

HOSTILE SHELLING.
Enemy shelled CAMBRIN this morning with 4.2 gun, also shelled LA BASSÉE road intermittently throughout the day nearly reaching the TOURIERS LOOP at one period.

WORK. At 7.25 am a German working party was seen near point 72 in A 30 c. soon after a tree was removed, presumably blown up.

At 7 am a flag pole was seen on case raising tower of FOSSE 8, later in the day it was noticed it had been removed.

Light has been good all day to day, the afternoon being exceptional.

R. Reeves 2/r
adj 41st Bde RFA

"A" Form.
Army Form C. 2121.

MESSAGES AND SIGNALS.

Prefix	Code	m.	Words	Charge	This message is on a/c of:	Recd. at ... m.
Office of Origin	Service Instructions		Sent			Date
			At ... m.			From
			To			By
			By		(Signature of "Franking Officer.")	

TO — I. RA. 2nd Divn.

| Sender's Number | Day of Month | In reply to Number | |
| OK/97 | 9½ | | AAA |

Daily Report 34th Bde. A Group.

50th Bty fired at 11.30 am } in retaliation for
3 pm } pip-squeaks. Fire
directed on SOUTH TOWPATH and
DOUBLE TRUCK.
At 5—5.20 pm on trenches in conjunction
with trench mortars.

70 Bty fired at 9.15 am, 10.15 am, 11.30 am, 1.5 pm,
and 3.35 pm in retaliation for small
how'r & pip-squeak fire on BRADDELL Pt,
HARLEY ST. & main road.
Fire directed on trenches in A1; on AUCHY—
LA BASSÉE road, on AUCHY—HAISNES road
& on batteries at A.17.d central, A.18.c.0.8.—
and A.18.a.6.6.
At 1.30 pm fired on working party A.21.b.8.5½
2.55 pm "   "   "   A.21.b.9.8.

56th Bty fired at 10.50 am } on working party
1.45 pm } A.16.a.2.3.

From
Place
Time

The above may be forwarded as now corrected.   (Z)

Censor.   Signature of Addressor or person authorised to telegraph in his name.
* This line should be erased if not required.

"A" Form. Army Form C. 2121.
MESSAGES AND SIGNALS. No. of Message..........

| Prefix...... Code........ m. | Words | Charge | This message is on a/c of: | Recd. at........ m. |
| Office of Origin Service Instructions. | Sent At........ m. To........ By........ | | ....Service. (Signature of "Franking Officer.") | Date.......... From.......... By.......... |

TO { II. RA. 2nd Divn

| Sender's Number. | Day of Month. | In reply to Number | AAA |
| OK/97. | 9th. | | |

7th Mountain Bty. — Between 2 & 3.30 pm. fired on trenches in A2 & TRIANGLE in retaliation.

(1) Observation impossible between 4.30 pm and 7. am.

(2) Enemy light how'rs & field guns were active today, firing down LA BASSÉE Road & HARLEY ST. PONT FIXE was shelled during the afternoon with 6" or 8".

(3) Flashes of field gun battery were observed on a true bearing of 87½° from HUN VIEW. Time between flash & report 7.3 seconds.

From..........
Place..........
Time..........

A. Durand
Adj. 34th Bde.

"A" Form.
MESSAGES AND SIGNALS. Army Form C. 2121.

Prefix	Code	m.	Words	Charge	This message is on a/c of:	Rec'd. at	m.
Office of Origin and Service Instructions.						Date	
			Sent		Service.	From	
			At	m.			
			To				
			By		(Signature of "Franking Officer.")	By	

TO { II.   R.A. 2nd Divn.

Sender's Number.	Day of Month.	In reply to Number	
* OK/114.	11th		AAA

Shelled today with 6" & 8" Hows from direction of SALOME and VIOLAINES.

Flashes of SALOME battery were seen several times — magnetic bearing 95° from A.15.c.1.9½.

The distillery walls & buildings near were damaged to a considerable extent.

59th Siege battery fired a dozen shell in retaliation —

Enemy fired between 400 - 500 shell.

A Durand Lt.

From
Place   Adj. 34th Bde.
Time

MESSAGES AND SIGNALS.

Army Form C. 2121.

TO 2nd Div G

Sender's Number: Hx 867   Day of Month: 11

Activity by enemy aaa 10 am to 11 am some intermittent field gun fire aaa 12 am to 4.30 pm heavy howitzer fire on PONT FIXE intermittent at first and intense at 2.30 and heavy till 4.30 aaa

From Place: Ra 2 Div

DAILY DIARY.

Z Group.   14.11.15.

9th Bat. Fired on new German work in FRANKS
    KEEP and on long stretch in A21 b 9 2.
    Dispersed working party in A23 A 04.
    Shelled A22 A 7 a in retaliation to
    minenwerfer at the request of infantry.
15th Bat. Fired on AUCHY several times dur-
    ing the day.
17th Bat. Searched along trench in rear of
    LES BRIQUES where working party was
    seen, fired on them again later.
    Fired on HAISNES in retaliation
47th Bat. Fired on FRANKS & RYANS KEEP
    in retaliation to minenwerfer.
48th Registered, and Retaliated on AUCHY.

All Batteries including the 11th Bty fired
    on German Batty A6a. according
    to pre arranged programme.

WORK.
    Germans are doing a lot of work
    strengthening trench in rear of LONE

DAILY AMMUNITION RETURN.

9. XI. 15

Piece	Projectile	Code	30	70	15	48	71	9	16	17	47	56			Total	Per Piece
18-pr	Guns															
	Shrapnel	A	48	24	81	-	76	182	78	72					561	
	H. E.	Ax	-	62	11	-	42	3	-	30					148	
4.5" (howzr)	Howitzers																
	Shrapnel	Z									19				19	
	H. E.	Zx								30	2				32	

1455

2nd Division Artillery Orders

by

Lieut.-Colonel C.R.P.PARRY, Comdg.R.A., 2nd Division.

9th November, 1915.

1098. TINS ETC., - RETURN OF

All empty oil drums and biscuit tins not required in the trenches are to be returned to D.A.D.O.S.

1099. HEAD ROPES.

1st Corps state that any chains required in lieu of hide head ropes will be issued on demand - there being no restriction as to the proportions of each kind to be held. (Authority,2nd Divn.No.Q.123/2.).

1100. WATER TROUGHS.

A sample water trough has been made on a pattern supplied by the R.E. As R.E. and Divisional Carpenters Workshop is fully occupied with other work, it will be necessary for R.A.Units to make up their own water troughs. O's.C.Units should send men down to Bomb Factory to do this. The sample water trough has been inspected by C.R.A., who considers it satisfactory in every way.

L.G.BUXTON, Capt, R.A.

Staff Captain, R.A., 2nd Div.

DAILY DIARY.

10.11.15

Z. Group.

9th Batt. Fired in retaliation to enemy shelling LA BASSE ROAD in CAMBRIN. Fired into AUCHY, A 21 d 10.7. also, both in retaliation.

15 Batt. Nothing to report.

17th Batt. Fired on enemy working party in their front line trench, at 1 pm and again at 2.50 pm. Fired on enemy trenches in retaliation.

47th Batt. Fired on german "Cooker" near A 28 b 16, in Retaliation to minenwerfer fired on RYANS KEEP, A 22 d 71 A 22 c 06 and FRANKS KEEP.

71st Batt. Fired on AUCHY in retaliation otherwise nothing to report.

ENEMY SHELLING.
Enemy shelled LA BASSE ROAD intermittenly throughout the

day, starting at Junction of HARLEY STREET right down to CROSS ROADS of TOURBIER'S LOOP, seemed to be fired from AUCHY.

Work. A machine Gun emplacement is suspected at A.22.d.2.4. No new work was noticed.

Observation was just possible this morning, Light was rely good this afternoon

Steam from an engine was seen in B.19.c. moving East by North.

LDReeks 2/L

Just reported
Adj' 41st Bde RFA

A small mine exploded at 6.10 pm on our left front; no further particulars yet. LDReeks

"A" Form.   **MESSAGES AND SIGNALS.**   Army Form C. 2121.

| TO | I | RA 2nd Divn | |

Sender's Number: OK/105. Day of Month: 10th.   AAA

Daily Report. 34th Bde.
A Group.

50th Bty — At 1.45 pm. fired on embankment in retaliation for shelling on CAMBRIN & slightly on front trenches in A2. On 9th:—

70th Bty — At 5.35 pm fired on trenches in A1 in retaliation for pip-squeaks on HARLEY ST.

On 10th:— At 9.40 am on AUCHY-HAISNES road in retaliation for shelling of BRADDELL POINT — and on trench mortar A.21.b.88. At 12.15 on movement seen on suspected observation ladder at A.18.b.10.0. It is believed that these are high tension posts on HAISNES-LA BASSEE road, & are used for observation. At 1.40 pm. & 3 pm. on AUCHY-HAISNES road in retaliation for pip-squeaks on CAMBRIN & main road.

7th Mountain Bty. — Did not fire —

MESSAGES AND SIGNALS.

"A" Form. — Army Form C. 2121.

| TO | II. | RA 2nd Divn. | |

Sender's Number.	Day of Month.	In reply to Number	
OK/105.	10th.		AAA

56th Bty. At 9.50 am. retaliated on to minenwerfer at request of infantry.
At 10.40 am retaliated to minenwerfer South of LA BASSEE road.
At 11.35 am. fired on field battery at abt. A.18.a.1.1. which was active.
At 9.30 am – 11 am & abt. 4 – 4.40. enemy shelled CAMBRIN & road.
Observation impossible from 4.30 pm 9th to 7 am 10th.

A Durand
Adj. 34th Bde.

SECRET.   2nd Division No. G.S. 711/1.

2nd Division.
No. 1/C.A./6(2).   9th Nov: 1915.

1.   With reference to this office No.1./C.A./6 dated 6th instant, wire-cutting will be begun by the 2nd and 7th Divisions this week.

   Please report to 1st Corps on what day and on what portions of the front the tasks will be carried out.

2.   Advantage should be taken of these occasions to instruct young Artillery Officers in the practice of wire-cutting.

                    (Sgd).   H. LEWIN. Major, for
                                   Brigadier-General,
                         General Staff, First Corps.

              2.

R.A.,
   2nd DIVISION.

   Reference above, please report to Divisional Headquarters the date and places you select.

                                        E. Davidson
2nd Divn: Captain.
10th Novr: 1915.   General Staff, 2nd Division.

DAILY AMMUNITION RETURN

DATE 10.XI.15

BATTERIES.

Piece	Projectile	Code	50	70	15	48	71	9	16	17	47	56	Total	Per Piece
18-pr	Guns......	48												
	Shrapnel...	"A"	28	35	47	-	35	54	101	16			316	
	H.E.......	"Ax"	11	39	19	-	45	79	2	66			261	
4.5"	Howitzers..													
	Shrapnel...	"B"									-	11	11	
	H.E.......	"Bx"									7	22	29	
7mn By		P											56	

2nd Division Artillery Orders

by

Lieut.-Colonel C.R.P.PARRY, Comdg. R.A., 2nd Division.

10th November, 1915.

1101. LEAVE.

Leave has been reduced to 24 men per day. Officers as before, namely 2 per day from Brigades and 1 from D.A.C., in order of Brigades.

New allotment as follows :-

Monday.	13 men.	-	36th Brigade.
	8 "	-	7th Mountain Bty.
	1 "	-	Armoured Cars.
	1 "	-	D.A.C.
	1 "	-	Spare.
Tuesday.	13 men.	-	41st Brigade.
	5 "	-	34th "
	3 "	-	44th "
	1 "	-	D.A.C.

Remaining days 22 men per day, instead of 28.

1102. HORSES - WATERING PLACES FOR

O's.C.Units will report by evening of 11th inst, the position by map square where their batteries and B.A.C's are now watering.

L.G.BUXTON, Capt, R.A.,
Staff Captain, R.A., 2nd Divn.

DAILY DIARY.

Z. Group.   11.11.15.

9th Batt. Fired on FRANKS KEEP in retaliation to enemy shelling CAMBRIN support trench. Fired on East side of NEW crater, made by mine exploding last evening, at the request of infantry.

15th Batt. Fired in retaliation on minenwerfer and HAISNES. Shelled house in AUCHY A23 c 61, completely destroyed later by 71st Batt: also fired on LONE FARM.

5th Batt. Fired on SNIPERS POST also on AUCHY and HAISNES. A new German work was observed at A29 a 86 and fired on, also a working party at A22 a 86

47th Batt. Nothing to report.

71st Batt. Fired on AUCHY, PEKIN. TRENCH ALLEY and PENTAGON during the day. Suspected O.P. A23 C 45 and fired on it. destroyed house A23 c 61.

HOSTILE SHELLING
   This morning enemy shelled CAMBRIN

Support trenches, later in the day we shelled PONTE FIXE and CUINCHY with 5-9 HE on percussion.

To day the enemy appear to have brought down 3 more trees at A30d46 and 2 more in A20c.
New shield in German front line trench in A21d77 was noticed to day also long posts for wire, put up during last night.
Smoke again seen from engine as reported yesterday.

Light to day was fairly good.

Reeves 2/r
9 adj 4th Bde RFA

"A" Form.
MESSAGES AND SIGNALS.

Army Form C. 2121.

Code. m.	Words	Charge	This message is on a/c of:	Recd. at m.
Orig'd Service Instructions.	Sent			Date
	At m.		Service.	From
	To			By
	By		(Signature of "Franking Officer.")	

TO	I.	R.A. 2nd Divn.		

Sender's Number.	Day of Month.	In reply to Number	AAA
OK/114.	11ᵗʰ		

<u>Daily Report</u> | A Group.

50ᵗʰ Bty. Fired between 12 & 1 pm. at distillery A.18.c.2.8, on trenches N of canal & on Embankment redoubt in retaliation for heavy How'r fire on PONT FIXE & pip-squeaks on the HOLLOW. Registered LA BASSEE - HAISNES road.

70ᵗʰ Bty. Have not fired.

7ᵗʰ Mountain Bty. Fired between 9 & 11 am. on trenches A.21.b.9.6 to Brickstacks, & on triangle.

56ᵗʰ Bty. Fired at 1.40 pm, 2.50 pm, 3.27 pm, on battery in action at A.18.a.0.1.

(1) Observation impossible from 4.15 pm. - 7.45 am.
(2) Light very good all day –
(3) PONT FIXE & vicinity was heavily

From
Place
Time

The above may be forwarded as now corrected. (Z)

RA 2nd Div.

Positions

As last week, but add

Sect. 7th Mountain Battery — Arbd 4.2

11.11.15

Mowbray
Major
BMRA

DAILY AMMUNITION RETURN

DATE 11. X. 15

B A T T E R I E S.

Piece	Projectile	Code	50	70	15	48	71	9	16	17	47	56	Total	Per Piece
18-pr	Guns.......	48												
	Shrapnel...	"A"	2	24	31	-	30	28	6	42	-	-	163	
	H. E.......	"Ax"	-	-	15	-	41	7	-	46	-	-	109	
4.5"	Howitzers..	12												
	Shrapnel...	"B"												
	H. E.......	"Bx"									8	-	8	
7th Mountn													42	

2nd Division Artillery Orders

by

Lieut-Colonel C.R.P.PARRY, Comdg. R.A., 2nd Division.

11th November, 1915.

1103. COURTMARTIAL.

A F.G.C.M., composed as under, will assemble at 10-0 a.m. on Saturday, 13th November, 1915, at Headquarters, 44th B.A.C., RUE GAMBETTA, BETHUNE for the purpose of trying No. 59011, Gr. J.Dixon, 15th Battery, R.F.A., and No.12376, Dr. L.Sams, 47th Battery, and such other accused as may be brought before them.

Accused to be warned and all witnesses duly required to attend.

Proceedings to be sent to this office.

PRESIDENT.
Major R.ff. Powell.   -   71st Battery, R.F.A.

MEMBERS.
Captain E.W.Griffiths. - 2nd Divnl. Ammn. Col.
Captain   Clark.   - H.Q., 1st Army.
Lieut. A.J.Wark.   - 17th Battery, R.F.A.

O.C.44th Bde. to detail a Court Orderly and the supply of necessary stationery.

1104. LORRIES.

It is particularly requested that Officers Commanding units will ensure that the parties working with the Slag lorries go to the right place and arrive punctually. Lorries are now provided by 2nd D.S.C. and can be relied on to be punctual.

L. G. BUXTON   Captain R.A.
Staff Captain 2nd Divisional Arty.

DAILY DIARY.

Z Group.   12.11.15.

9th Batt. Fired 6 rounds per hour on New East side of new crater, as arranged with infantry. Dispersed party of about 60 Germans in B 13.d 07, also a working party in B 18 c 33. Twice fired on German 2nd Line Trench.

15th Batt. Retaliated on AUCHY. and checked several targets.

17th Batt. Registered A 29 a 13 where Germans have been strengthening their line, nothing to report.

4th Batt. Fired on RYANS KEEP in retaliation to minenwerfer also at A 27 d 71 later

48th Batt to-day relieved the 71st Batt.

HOSTILE SHELLING.
The enemy to-day shelled the 17th Batt at the North end of TOUBIERS LOOP. also shelled A 25 d 55, with 5.9 HE.
Also shelled our trenches south

of VERMELLES-LABASSEE ROAD

WORK.
Enemy are putting up new stakes in FRANKS KEEP.
Fresh German work observed at A29 a 78, apparently they are making this place very strong as a great deal of new earth has been thrown up, and much work has been noticed there lately.

Light during the day was very changeable being quite good for short periods.

LR Reeves 2/L
9adj 41st Bde

"A" Form.
Army Form C. 2121.

MESSAGES AND SIGNALS.

| TO | 2nd Div GS |

Sender's Number.	Day of Month	In reply to Number	
BM 875	12		AAA

Activity by enemy aaa 2.30 to 4 pm TOURBIERES LOOP N branch and railway in A 75 d 5.9 and 4.2 inch aaa In yesterdays shelling enemy threw nearly 500 shell into PONT FIXE at one time at 8 a minute aaa Damage very slight rumoured to by 5 men wounded aaa

From Ra 7 Div
Place
Time 7 pm

DAILY DIARY.

Z. Group.   13.11.15.

9th Batt. Fired on A 21 B 9½ 4 where stakes
   were seen to be new. Otherwise nothing
   to report
15th Batt. Fired on LONE FARM.
17th Batt. Noticed timber being carried into
   house A 30 d 05 and fired on same.
47th Batt. Nothing to report.
8th Batt. Registered targets which were
   visible.

HOSTILE SHELLING
         Already reported.

Germans were seen to be baling out
   their trench in several places.
Craters appear to be settling down owing
to the bad weather.
Germans sent up 7 single white
lights from 8.45 am to 11-30 am from
A 28 d 17.
   Light has not been good to day
                          U. Reeves 2/Lt
                       adj 41st Bde RFA.

Copy No............

2ND DIVISION OPERATION ORDER No. 74.

Reference Map - BETHUNE Combined Sheet,
1/40,000.

11th November, 1915.

1. 19th Infantry Brigade will be relieved in "A" Section by 22nd Infantry Brigade, 7th Division on the 12th and 13th November under arrangements made direct between Brigade Commanders concerned.

19th Infantry Brigade will relieve 5th Infantry Brigade in "Z" Section on 12th and 13th November, under arrangements made direct between Brigade Commanders concerned.

Northern boundary of 2nd Division will be THE LANE (exclusive) - CAMBRIN SUPPORT POINT - TOURBIERES and CARTERS REDOUBTS (all inclusive), thence along main road to HEDGEROW LANE (exclusive), thence excluding LE PREOL and LE QUESNOY and including BEUVRY to the Canal at F.1.d.0.0.

2. 6th Infantry Brigade will relieve 36th Infantry Brigade, 12th Division from SAVILE ROW (exclusive) to R.1 on the 13th and 14th November, under arrangements made direct between Brigade Commanders concerned.

Southern boundary of 2nd Division will be GORDON ALLEY - BOYAU 12 - SAVILE ROW (all exclusive) - CENTRAL KEEP - FOUNTAIN KEEP (both inclusive) - BULLY KEEP (exclusive), thence to FOSSE COTTAGES, ANNEQUIN (exclusive), and BEUVRY (inclusive)

3. Relief of battalions will be carried out in accordance with the attached March Table.

4. R.A., 2nd Division will place that part of the Divisional Artillery now covering the front GUN STREET - CANAL (three 18-pdr. batteries and one 4.5" How. battery) at the disposal of 7th Division.

The 12th Division is placing that part of its Divisional Artillery now covering the front SAVILE ROW - R.1 (five 18-pdr. batteries and one 4.5" How. battery) at the disposal of 2nd Division.

Batteries will be transferred and responsibility for the artillery support of the fronts to be taken over will be assumed at hours to be arranged direct between Divisional Artillery Commanders concerned, the time being notified to Divisional Headquarters.

5. 5th Field Company, R.E. will remain in Section "Z" and will be affiliated for work to 19th Infantry Brigade.

11th Field Company, R.E. will be affiliated for work to 6th Infantry Brigade.

6. No.6 Trench Mortar Battery will remain in "Z" Section, and will be attached to 19th Infantry Brigade.

1 section No.62 Trench Mortar Battery now in "A" Section will be withdrawn from the trenches on 12th instant., will be billetted with 34th Brigade A.C. and attached to 6th Infantry Brigade.

1 section No.62 Trench Mortar Battery now attached 6th Infantry Brigade will be at disposal of 6th Infantry Brigade for work in the trenches.

Arrangements for transport of these sections will be made direct between 19th Infantry Brigade and R.A., 2nd Division and 6th Infantry Brigade and R.A., 2nd Division respectively.

7. 2nd Division will hand over the evacuation of "A" Section and will take over the evacuation of the new line under arrangements to be made direct between A.D's.M.S., 2nd 7th and 12th Divisions.

8. The command of the various sections will be handed over and taken over by Brigade Commanders on completion of reliefs of the front line, and a report sent to Divisional Headquarters.

9. Report Centre unchanged.

J.B. Belgrave, Major,
General Staff, 2nd Division.

Issued at 7.30 pm to:-

Copy No.1.... 5th Infantry Brigade.
,, 2.... 6th Infantry Brigade.
,, 3.... 19th Infantry Brigade.
,, 4.... R.A., 2nd Division.
,, 5.... R.E., 2nd Division.
,, 6.... Divisional Mounted Troops.
,, 7.... No.1 Bty. M.M.G.Service.
,, 8.... Divisional Signal Company.
,, 9.... A.D.M.S.
,, 10.... A.P.M.
,, 11.... "Q".
,, 12.... 2nd Divisional Train.
,, 13 &
   14... 1st Corps.   )
,, 15.... 7th Division.   )
,, 16.... 12th Division.   )
,, 17.... 180th Tunnelling Company,R.E) For information.
,, 18.... 251st   ,,   ,, ,,)
,, 19.... 186th Special Co. R.E.   )
,, 20 to
   24... G.S. and record.

MARCH TABLE.

(Issued with 2nd Div: Operation Order No 74)

Date.	Unit.	From.	To.	Remarks.
12th November.	5th Inf.Bde. 1 battalion.	CAMBRIN.	BETHUNE.(Ecole de Jeunes Filles)	
	19th " Bde. " "	BEUVRY.	ANNEZIN.	) On relief by 7th Division
	" " " "	BEUVRY.	CAMBRIN.	) Reserve Bns of 19th Bde will come
	" " " "	Front Line.	BEUVRY.	) temporarily under command of G.O.C 22nd Bde
	" " " "	Front Line.	BEUVRY.	)
13th November.	5th Inf.Bde. 1 battalion.	Front Line.	BEUVRY.	
	" " " "	Front Line.	BETHUNE.(Rue d'Aire)	
	" " " "	BETHUNE.(Ecole de Jeunes Filles).	GONNEHEM.	
	19th Inf.Bde. "	HARLEY STREET and support points	Front Line.	) Section "Z". Relief of
	" " " "	ANNEQUIN.	Front Line.	) 5th Brigade.
	" " " "	BEUVRY.	BETHUNE (Fouillard Barracks.)	
	6th Inf.Bde. "	BETHUNE. (Fouillard Barracks)	Fosse Cottages. (ANNEQUIN).	
	" "	BETHUNE. (Rue d'Aire.)	SAILLY LA BOURSE.	) On arrival will come under
	" "	BUSNETTES.	BETHUNE.(Ecole de Jeunes Filles.)	) orders of 12th Division
	" "	GONNEHEM.	ANNEQUIN.	) temporarily.
14th November.	6th Inf.Bde. "	Fosse Cottages. (ANNEQUIN)	Front Line.	
	" "	SAILLY LA BOURSE.	Front Line.	) In relief of 36th Brigade.
	" "	BETHUNE. (Feuillard Barracks)	Support Trenches.	

(2).

MARCH TABLE. (Continued)

Date.	Unit.		From.	To.	Remarks.
14th November.	8th Inf.Bde.	1 battalion.	BETHUNE.(Ecole de Jeunes Filles)	BEUVRY.	
	,,	,,	GONNEHEM.	BETHUNE. ANNEQUIN. Rest Area:- ANNEZIN. VENDIN. GONNEHEM. BUSNETTES.	
	5th Inf.Bde.		VENDIN.		

"A" Form. Army Form C. 2121.
MESSAGES AND SIGNALS.

TO 2nd Div G

At 4 pm 17th RA assumes command of left group 12th Div RA as follows.

HQ	64th Bde	L5 b 6.10	
64th Bde			
	A	A25 b 6.10	
	B	A25 b 1.8	
	C	A19 d 1.1	
	D	A25 b 1.9	
63rd Bde			
	D	A25 b 1.6	
62nd Bde			
	A	A14 c 2.6	

"A" Form.　　　　　　　　　　　　　　　　　　　Army Form C. 2121.
MESSAGES AND SIGNALS.　　　　　　　　　　　No. of Message _____

Prefix	Code	m.	Words	Charge	This message is on a/c of:	Recd. at _____ m.
Office of ___ and Service Instructions.			Sent		_____ Service.	Date _____
			At _____ m.			From _____
			To _____			
			By _____		(Signature of "Franking Officer.")	By _____

TO

Sender's Number.	Day of Month	In reply to Number	A A A

Observing Stations

A	64	G3a9.0 PHALLOS	G3C89 Block Ho.
B	64	A27a centr	LONDON
C	64	A20d68	LANDS END
D	64	A27a86	BEN MACDUI
A	62	A20d48	
D	55	A27a55	LE GHEER

From　Ra?Dn
Place　4.15pm
Time

The above may be forwarded as now corrected.　(Z)　_____
　　　　　　　　　　　　　　　　　　　　　　　　　　Maj
Censor.　　　　　　　　　　　Signature of Addressor or person authorised to telegraph in his name.

* This line should be erased if not required.

DAILY AMMUNITION RETURN

DATE 12.XI.15.

BATTERIES.

Piece	Projectile	Code	50	70	15	48	71	9	16	17	47	56	Total Per Piece
18-pr	Guns.......												
	Shrapnel...	"A"	24	-	29	-	49	75	-	53	-	-	230
	H. E.......	"Ax"	3	-	-	-	76	14	-	33	-	-	126
4.5"	Howitzers..												
	Shrapnel...	"B"											
	H. E.......	"Bx"									2	31	33

2nd Divisional Artillery Orders

By

Lieutenant-Colonel C. R. P. Parry, Commanding R.A., 2nd Divn.

12th November, 1915.

1105. **DAMAGES TO BILLETS.**

The G.O.C., 2nd Diviton directs that units billetted at ANNEQUIN and CAMBRIN take adequate steps to put a stop once and for all to the ruthless destruction of houses and other shelter, all of which are most necessary for accommodation.

1106. **LEAVE - WARRANTS.**

All Leave passes and Tickets are to be clearly endorsed with the route by which the holder is to travel viz either via BOULOGNE-FOLKESTONE or via HAVRE-SOUTHAMPTON.

1107. **EQUIPMENT - SADDLES.**

All off-saddles should be returned to Ordnance. This saddlery should be properly packed in sacks and labelled as follows :-

"Returned from........th Battery under authority 1st Army O.S.43/9"

They should be returned to D.A.D.O.S. at refilling point. Only one unit will return saddles per day, and dates are allotted as follows :-

50th Battery,	14th Nov.	9th Battery,	21st. Nov.
70th ,,	15th	16th ,,	22nd.
34th B.A.C.	16th	17th ,,	23rd.
15th Battery	17th	41st B.A.C.	24th.
48th ,,	18th	47th Battery	25th.
71st ,,	19th	56th ,,	26th.
36th B.A.C.	20th	44th B.A.C.	27th.
2nd Divl.Ammn.Col.	28th.		

1108. **RE-ENLISTMENT, EXTENSION OF SERVICE, ETC.**

Copies of an extract from General Routine Orders dated 10th November 1915, are issued herewith for information and communication to all ranks concerned.

L. G. BUXTON Captain R.A.

Staff Captain R. A. 2nd Dn.

"A" Form.   Army Form C. 2121.

MESSAGES AND SIGNALS.

Prefix ____ Code ____ m. | Words | Charge | This message is on a/c of: | Recd. at ____ m.
Office of Origin and Service Instructions. | Sent | | | Date ____
| At ____ m. | | Service. | From ____
| To ____ | | |
| By ____ | | (Signature of "Franking Officer.") | By ____

TO   Ra 7 Div

Sender's Number: BM 876   Day of Month: 13   In reply to Number: AAA

Enemy have taken down three more trees at A30d 4.6 and two more at A20c aaa There is a new shield in front line trench at A21d 7.7 aaa There are also some new long posts for wire there aaa Fresh work has been seen at A29d 7.8 where much earth has been thrown up aaa Battery has been located from (1/10000) A18a 0.1 to 1.1 aaa This will be dealt with combined fire when it reopens aaa Working party at B13d 0.7 and at B15c 3.3 dispersed aaa Some work done at A29a 1.3 aaa 48th Battery has relieved the 7th aaa.

From: Ra 7 Div
Place:
Time: 9 am

(Z)   Mowbray Major

1470

DAILY AMMUNITION RETURN

DATE 13 Nov. 1915.

BATTERIES.

Piece	Projectile	Code	50	70	15	48	71	9	16	17	47	56	Total	Per Piece
18-pr	Guns.......	48												
	Shrapnel...	"A"	31	-	24	25	-	34	36	49	-	-	199	
	H. E.......	"Ax"	4	-	3	8	-	20	-	5	-	-	40	
4.5"	Howitzers..	12												
	Shrapnel...	"B"										3	3	
	H. E.......	"Bx"									4	2	6	

2nd Division Artillery Orders

by

Lieut-Colonel C.R.P.PARRY, Commanding R.A., 2nd Division.

13th November, 1915.

1109. DIVINE SERVICE.

Divine Service tomorrow for units in or near BETHUNE at 10-0 a.m. in unfinished Chapel, Rue d'Aire.

Divine Service tomorrow for batteries in action at TOURBIERES cross roads A.19.d.0.3. at 11-30 a.m.

1110. LIMBERS & AMMUNITION WAGONS - REPAIR OF

If it is necessary to send any Limbers or Ammunition Wagons to Ordnance Workshops for repair, all Gun ammunition must be removed first.

1111. HURDLES.

All hurdles not actually in use for revetting, or as proper windscreens, are to be returned to the hurdle depot at BEUVRY.

1112. LEAVE.

From tomorrow, sunday night inclusive, N.C.O's. and men proceeding on leave will assemble at the Rest Billet next door to Orphanage,(1st turn to left from the Rue MICHELET) prior to being marched to the station, and not at the Recreation Room, Rue d'Aire, as heretofore.

The leave Conducting Officer will parade the party outside the building at 10-45 p.m. and march them to the station.

1113. DETENTION ALLOWANCE.

Officers returning to the Expeditionary Force from, leave or duty in England who are held up through military exigencies at a port of embarkation may be allowed the regulated rates of detention allowance for the period they are necessarily detained. (Authority, W.O., letter No.14/Miscellaneous/342, d/5/11/1915.)

L.G.BUXTON, Capt,R.
Staff Captain, R.A.2/Divn.

General Information
C/64th Bde R.F.A.

By whom reported	Time	Information
2/Lt George Bateman	12.0 to 3.30 p.m.	A number of men wearing grey uniforms & caps were seen coming out of HAINES ALLEY at A.24.c.9½ & cross the open into HAISNES. These were fired at at intervals, the men being seen to run. At 2.15 a party of fifteen passed this point, they wore the same grey uniform but carried full pack & rifle.
	2.30 pm	Three men were shovelling earth out of the CORD. The work continued during the afternoon.

14.11.15.

Capt.
P. Barton
Major R.A.

15-11-15

T.R.M. considerable amount wire has been put up at stakes A31692. Fresh earthwork was also noticed in FRANKS KEEP.

Observation was possible between 10 A.M. and 4 P.M., between these hours it was good.

L. Reams 2/Lt
7 adj 41st Bde R.F.A.

S E C R E T.   2nd Division No, G.S. 711/2.

2nd Division.

No.1/C.A./6(3).   14th November, 1915.

Reference 1st Corps No. 1/C.A./6 dated 8th instant, wire cutting is to commence this week. Divisions will report to Corps Headquarters date, time and position of proposed wire-cutting.

If, for certain reasons, Divisions wish to postpone this wire-cutting, they will report to Corps Headquarters, stating fully what these reasons are.

(Sd) J.K.DICK CUNYNGHAM.   Major,
for Brig-General,
General Staff, 1st Corps.

(2)

R.A., 2nd Division.

For information.

Please let me know what you propose with reference to the above.

E Davidson

2nd Division.   Captain,
14th November, 1915.   General Staff, 2nd Division.

1474

DAILY AMMUNITION RETURN

DATE 4. XI. 15.

BATTERIES.

Piece	Projectile	Code	50	70	15	48	71	9	16	17	47	56	Total	Per Piece
18-pr	Guns.......													
	Shrapnel...	"A"	142	-	26	51	-	2	64	8	-	-	293	
	H.E.......	"Ax"	85	39	-	11	-	36	32	57	-	-	260	
4.5"	Howitzers..													
	Shrapnel...	"B"											-	
	H.E.......	"Bx"								10	78	-	88	

DAILY DIARY

Z Group.   15.11.15

9th Batt. Fired occasional rounds during the night on new wire FRANKS KEEP, otherwise nothing to report.

15th Batt. Fired on HAISNES, otherwise nothing to report.

17th Batt. Retaliated on AUCHY and also on German trenches.

47th Batt. Fired on Cross Roads A 23 c 9 2 in retaliation to German shelling with 77mm on HARLEY STREET.

48th Batt. Fired into HAISNES at 6.am. later on a O.P. in AUCHY in retaliation.

No new work was noticed to day.

Light was good most of the day.

D. Reeves 2/L
Adj 41st Bde R.F.A.

"A" Form. Army Form C. 2121.

MESSAGES AND SIGNALS.

Prefix	Code	m.	Words	Charge	This message is on a/c of:	Recd. at	m.
Office of Origin and Service Instructions.			Sent		Service.	Date	
			At	m.		From	
			To				
			By		(Signature of "Franking Officer.")	By	

TO 2nd Div G

Sender's Number.	Day of Month	In reply to Number	A A A
Bm 889	15		

Hostile Shelling

8.15	to 8.40	15 rounds	77 mm HE on	A27a 87
8.30	to 9.30	25	59 m.	A20 b 6.5
9		10	77 mm	A27a
9.30	to 10	35	77 mm	A27 b 24
9 / 2			100 mm How	Harley St.
1.30 – 2.30		50	77 mm	A20 d 19
2 – 4.30		intermittent	15 cm How	Vermelles Sta.

From Ra 2 Div
Place
Time 7 pm

"A" Form.   Army Form C. 2121.

MESSAGES AND SIGNALS.   No. of Message_____

Prefix____Code____m.	Words	Charge	This message is on a/c of:	Recd. at____m.
Office of Origin and Service Instructions.				Date_____
	Sent			
	At____m.		____Service.	From_____
	To____			
	By____		(Signature of "Franking Officer")	By____

TO — { A.A. 2nd Div. G

Sender's Number	Day of Month	In reply to Number	
BM 8814	15		AAA

RA assumed command of Left Group
7 Div Artillery on 14th at 9 pm
aaa 41st Brigade took part in combined
shoot on a battery accurately located
at A 18 a 0.1 at 11 am aaa working
party at A 23 a 0.9 dispersed aaa Enemy
are doing much work strengthening
trench E of LONE FARM aaa new wire has been
put up at A 21 b 9.2 aaa

From   RA 7 Div
Place
Time   9 am

The above may be forwarded as now corrected.   (Z)
                                       Censor.   Brig. Major
                                                  Signature of Addressor or person authorised to telegraph in his name
* This line should be erased if not required.

DAILY AMMUNITION RETURN

DATE 15.XI.15

BATTERIES.

Piece	Projectile	Code	50	70	15	48	71	9	16	17	47	56	Total Per Piece
18-pr	Guns......												
	Shrapnel...	"A"	98	3	17	99	-	85	15	34	-	-	351
	H.E.......	"Ax"	-	16	16	59	-	96	-	34	-	-	221
4.5"	Howitzers..												
	Shrapnel...	"B"											-
	H.E.......	"Bx"										18	39	57

[146]

General Information 14.11.15

I. The Germans today were exposing themselves in the area A 28, 29 much more than usual — Small parties were seen in the open on more than one occasion - dress could not be seen in detail - about 11.30 am a German was reported to have shewn himself from the waist up in the front line at Railway trench — The same occurred at 2.30 pm but I am inclined to think it was a dummy from the short glance I had at it —

II. A new trench is apparently being dug and wire put up along the S. side of the Railway near A 28 b 5. ½ northwards — In that neighbourhood wire generally seems to be increasing

III. Redoubts or similar mounds seem to be increasing in trench A 30 c 7.0 — 10.6 especially about 8½.7½

IV. The mound about the junction of LITTLE WILLIE and new trench running to MAD POINT has a loophole A — 8 d 1½.2 facing N.W. and appears to be a machine gun emplacement flanking the latter trench

P Harlow Major RFA
15-11-15

H Kennedy Capt RFA
Clg D/64.

2nd Division Artillery Orders

by

Colonel A. EARDLEY WILMOT, Commanding R.A., 2nd Divn.

15th November, 1915.

1114. R.A. ORDERS.

Were not issued yesterday, 14th November, 1915.

1115. POSTING.

Lieutenant A. ANDERSON PELHAM from D.A.C. to command 36th B.A.C., vice FLETCHER (Sick to England) with effect from 26th October, 1915.

1116. LEAVE.

New allotment for leave which is open again:-

Tuesday.	-	15 men.	-	36th Brigade.
		9 "	-	7th Mountain Bty.
		1 "	-	Armoured Cars.
		3 "	-	D.A.C.
		1 "	-	Spare.
Wednesday.	-	15 men.	-	41st Brigade.
		7 "	-	34th "
		5 "	-	44th "
		1 "	-	D.A.C.
Thursday.	-	28 men.	-	34th Brigade.
Friday.	-	28 "	-	36th "
Saturday.	-	28 "	-	41st "
Sunday.	-	28 "	-	44th "
Monday.	-	28 "	-	D.A.C.

Allotment will continue on this scale until further orders. Officers as before.

1117. PERSONNEL.

O.C. Units should report by 6 p.m. 16th inst whether all or any of the following men are serving in their units. Nil reports are not necessary, and if no reports are received by 6 p.m. a nil reply will be sent to 2nd Divn. Numbers are not known. -
Gunners CROOK. COPLAND. & HASKELL.

L.C. BUXTON., Capt, R.A.,
Staff Captain, R.A., 2nd Divn.

DAILY DIARY.

Z group.   Nov 16th

9th Batt. fired on party sapping NE of ETNA
10 am. Retaliated at 12·49 after
a few rounds a dense volume
of white smoke was seen from
crater opp. point D but no ex-
-plosion was heard. Fired at
2pm on suspected O.P. on german
heavies shelling our second line
Floor colapsed and house is now
flat. Fired on German tr. Mor.
near pt. 51

15th Batt. fired seven times in retaliation
on POPES nose MINE pt. & railway
line.

17th Batt fired on periscope in front
tr. and on Germans working
there at 2·15pm and 3·30pm when
they were mending parapet.

47th How. Batt fired four rounds on
FRANKS heap & a 21d 7l. in reply
to MINENWERFER 3·30pm

48th Batt fired four times in
retaliation on MINE pt. etc. 4·30pm
fired 12 rds into HAINES.

Germans required a good deal of retaliation today. They shelled SAMS peep as usual.

A large cloud of white smoke as reported from new crater as above.

Light had all day.

F. Todd
Adj: 41st Bde.

"A" Form.
Army Form C. 2121.
MESSAGES AND SIGNALS.
No. of Message _____

Prefix ___ Code ___ m.	Words	Charge	This message is on a/c of:	Recd. at ___ m.
Office of Origin and Service Instructions.	Sent At ___ m. To ___ By ___		___ Service. (Signature of "Franking Officer.")	Date ___ From ___ By ___

TO — 2nd Div G

Sender's Number.	Day of Month	In reply to Number	
BM 892	16		A A A

Activity by enemy areas.

15th Nov.	3.30 – 5.30	Steady bombardment 15 cm howitzer
		G4C & BARTS
16th	5 am – 6 am	10	77 mm	PONT FIXE
	10 – 11	20	77 mm	
			10 cm }	RAILWAY
			15 cm }	ALLEY
				HUMANITY
	3 pm – 5 pm		77 mm }	Support line
			10 cm }	& VERMELLES
			15 cm }	RAILWAY

From RA 2 Div
Place
Time 6.55 pm

The above may be forwarded as now corrected.
(Z) A Mackay
Censor. Signature of Addresser or person authorised to telegraph in his name.

* This line should be erased if not required.

DAILY AMMUNITION RETURN

DATE 16.XI.15.

BATTERIES.

Piece	Projectile	Code	50	70	15	48	71	9	16	17	47	56	Total	Per Piece
18-pr	Guns......													
	Shrapnel...	"A"	51	25	52	91	-	35	58	20	-	-	332	
	H.E.......	"Ax"	-	76	17	38	-	29	-	14	-	-	124	
4.5"	Howitzers..													
	Shrapnel...	"B"									-	-		
	H.E.......	"Bx"									6	13	19	

2nd Division Artillery Orders

by

Brigadier General G.H.SANDERS, Comdg. R.A., 2nd Division.

16th November, 1915.

1118. LEAVE - ALTERATION OF

Men of to-day's allotment will proceed to-morrow. All others will proceed one day later.

1119. WATER TROUGHS.

(a). O's.C.Units requiring connecting pipes for Watering Troughs should send an N.C.O., with means of conveyance to Headquarters, R.A., 2nd Division.

(b). Lieut. HAMBLYN, 5th Field Co., R.E., will, as far as possible visit all wagon lines, B.A.C. and D.A.C., to give advice on the making of water troughs. Officers or N.C.O's in charge of wagon lines should be warned that he may come and should give him every assistance.

L.G.BUXTON, Capt, R.A.,

Staff Captain, R.A., 2nd Division.

- NOTICE. -

LOST. - from 48th Battery, R.F.A., Wagon Line. - Bay Mare, height 15-3, blind near eye. - Marked, off hind 48, near hind 158.
Any information to be sent to O.C., 36th Brigade, R.F.A.

2nd Division Artillery Summary.

November 17th, 1915.

Position of guns located.

Nil.

Flashes.

Nil.

Hostile Artillery fire

No.	Time.	Nature.	Target.	From.	Remarks.
1.	8-0 a.m.	77m.m.	Trenches Z.1.		
2.	9-15a.m.	77m.m.	A.27.b.2.5.		to 10.5. a.m.
3.	10-30a.m.	105m.m.	A.14.b.3.1.		to 12-30 p.m.
4.	10-45a.m.	15c.m.	PONT FIXE.		10 rounds to 11-30 a.m.
5.	11-30a.m.) 1-30p.m.) 3-30p.m.)	77m.m.	Support trenches A.27.b. & A.28.c.		a few odd rounds.
6.	12-45p.m.	77m.m.	A.15.d.1.0.		till 1-15p.m.
7.	2-0 p.m.	77m.m.	VERMELLES.		
8.	3-0 p.m.	77m.m.	CAMBRIN.		

Enemy generally quiet.

Work done.

More stakes put up in rear of 1st line in A.21.d. last night. No wire on them.

                                          Major, R.A.,
Brigade Major, R.A., 2/Divn.

Copies to :-
     2nd Division. G.
     R.A., 1st Corps.
     R.A., 7th Division.
     R.A., 12th Division.
     H.A., 1st Corps.
     34th Brigade.
     36th   "
     41st   "
     44th   "

SECRET.

2nd Division.   IVth Corps.   Adv. First Army.
7th Division.   XIth Corps.
12th Division.   No.3 Squadron R.F.C.
33rd Division.   Heavy Artillery, 1st Corps.

2nd DIVISION
GENERAL STAFF
No. GS 712/1
Date. 18/11/15

No.G.153.   17th November, 1915.

---

1. With reference to 1st Corps Operation Order No.118 of 16th November, 1915, Artillery Reliefs between the 1st, 4th and 11th Corps will take place as under.

2. **Between 1st and 4th Corps.**
   (a). The artillery of the 15th Division will relieve that portion of the artillery of the 12th Division now covering the front held by the 12th Division on the nights 22nd/23rd and 23rd/24th November, under arrangements to be made between the Division concerned.

   (b). One section of each battery of the 12th Division now under the orders of the 2nd Division will be withdrawn from action on the night 23rd/24th November.
   The other section of each battery will be withdrawn on the night 24th/25th November, after the G.O.C., 15th Division has taken over command of his new front.
   From this hour the artillery of the 2nd Division will cover the new front of its own Division, i.e. from MUD TRENCH (exclusive) to WILLOW ROAD (A.9.d.44).

   (c). Batteries of the 12th Division, as relieved or withdrawn from action, will march into their reserve area under divisional arrangements.

3. **Between 1st and 11th Corps.**
   The artillery of the 7th Division will relieve the artillery of the 19th Division covering the front GRENADIER ROAD - LA QUINQUE RUE on the nights 22nd/23rd and 23rd/24th November, under arrangements to be made between the Divisions concerned.
   On completion of the relief the artillery of the 7th Division will cover the whole of the new front to be held by the 7th Division, i.e. from WILLOW ROAD (A.9.d.44) to LA QUINQUE RUE.

4. Completion of reliefs will be reported to 1st Corps.

(Sgd) J.K.Dick Cunyingham.   Major.
for Brigadier-General.
General Staff, 1st Corps.

2.

R.A., 2nd Division.

For information with reference to Operation Order No. 75.

                                              E. Davidson
2nd Divn: Captain.

18th November, 1915.   General Staff, 2nd Division.

"A" Form.
Army Form C. 2121.
MESSAGES AND SIGNALS.

No. of Message: 1181

TO: 2nd Div G

Sender's Number: BM 898
Day of Month: 17
AAA

Proposals for wire cutting aaa 64th Brigade Thursday 18th 1 pm at A28d2.1 A28c8.5 and A28a1.1 aaa 41st Brigade Friday 19th A27b 7.9 – 7.7 beginning when light is suitable aaa

From: RA 2nd Div
Place:
Time: 9.50 pm

1482

DAILY AMMUNITION RETURN

DATE 17. XI. 15

BATTERIES.

Piece	Projectile	Code	50	70	15	48	71	9	16	17	47	56	Total Per Piece
18-pr	Guns.......												
	Shrapnel...	"A"	5	16	96	115	-	36	22	4	-	-	294
	H. E.......	"Ax"	-	6	34	15	-	124	-	55	-	-	234
4.5"	Howitzers..												
	Shrapnel...	"B"										4	4
	H. E.......	"Bx"									4	41	45

2nd Division Artillery Orders

by

Brigadier-General G.H.SANDERS,   D.S.O., Comdg. R.A.,2/Divn.

17th November,1915.

1120. BATHS.

(a) The Baths in BEUVRY can be used by R.A.Units in that neighbourhood by application to the G.O.C., Infantry Brigade of the Northern Section, billeted at A.19.d.5.4.

(b) JEUNES FILLES SCHOOL Baths are allotted to R.A., 2nd Division on 19th instant as follows:-

8-30 to 10-0 a.m.	-	36th Brigade.
10-0 to 11-30 a.m.	-	41st "
11-30 to 1-0 p.m.	-	34th "
1-30 to 3-30 p.m.	-	D.A.C.
3-30 to 5-0 p.m.	-	44th Brigade.

Men should arrive in parties of 70 each half hour, and must bring their own soap and towels.   It is essential that each party is punctual.

L.G.BUXTON, Capt, R.A.

Staff Captain, R.A., 2nd Division.

DAILY AMMUNITION RETURN

DATE 18.XI.15.

BATTERIES.

Piece	Projectile	Code	50	70	15	48	71	9	16	17	47	56	Total Per Piece
18-pr	Guns.......												
	Shrapnel...	"A"	67	10	15	97	–	44	–	33	–	–	266
	H.E.......	"Ax"	–	6	4	30	–	98	–	13	–	–	151
4.5"	Howitzers..												
	Shrapnel...	"B"									–	–	–
	H.E.......	"Bx"									–	2	2

2nd Divisional Artillery Summary.

Position of Guns located.

    N I L.

Flashes located.

    N I L.

Hostile Artillery Fire.

No.	Time	Nature	Target	From direction of	Remarks.
1	9.20 a	77 mm	A 21 d 5/8 5	-	20 rounds.
2	9-45 a	77 mm	Russell's Koop	-	12 ,,
3	1-30 p to 2-10 p	77 mm	,,	-	20 ,,
4	2 & 2-30	77 mm	A 27 a 8½ 6½	AUCHY	2 rds @ 1 min interval.
5	2-15 p	77 mm	PONT FIXE	-	2 salvoes of 4 rounds.
6	2-30 p	77 mm	VERMELLES rd.	-	25 rounds.

Enemy quiet in spite of our wire cutting.

Our Artillery Fire.

From 1 to 4-15 p.m. 400 rounds fired on wire at A 28 d 2 2 Light too bad at conclusion to judge effect, but the shooting appeared good.

Other fire in retaliation.

New work.

Nothing observed.

G E N E R A L.

Light poor all day.
It is reported by an observer that LONE FARM is wrongly placed on the map (1/10000) and should be at A 29 a 1½ 3¼.

                                             Major R.A.
                               Brigade Major R.A. 2nd Divn.

"A" Form. Army Form C. 2121.

MESSAGES AND SIGNALS.

TO 2nd Div G

Sender's Number.	Day of Month	In reply to Number	A A A
Am 900	18		

Weekly report on positions aaa

x 50 Battery	F18a 4.4	
x 70	F24c 9.4	
15	(4)	G8a 0.5
48	(4)	F24c 8.9
x 9	F18c 4.1	
7	F24a 7.1	
7 mm	A26d 5.2	
A 62	A16c 2.6	
A 64	A25b 1.7	
B by	A25b 1.8	
C by	A19d 1.1	
D by	A25b 1.9	
D 65	A25b 1.6	

x Attached 7th Div

From RA 7 Div
Place
Time 2.15 pm

Munby Major

Copy No........ 5

2ND DIVISION OPERATION ORDER No. 75.

18th November, 1915.

Reference Map - BETHUNE Combined Sheet,
1/40,000.

1. On 22nd November 5th Infantry Brigade will take over the front from GUN STREET (inclusive) to WILLOW ROAD (A.9.d.4.4) from 22nd Brigade, 7th Division, under arrangements to be made direct between Brigade Commanders concerned.

2. On 23rd November, 6th Infantry Brigade will hand over the front from SAVILE ROW to HUD TRENCH (inclusive) to 46th Infantry Brigade, 15th Division, and will take over the front from R.1 to GUN STREET (exclusive) from 19th Infantry Brigade under arrangements to be made direct between Brigade Commanders concerned.

3. On relief, 19th Infantry Brigade will move into rest area, BUSNETTES, GONNEHEM, VENDIN, ANNEZIN.

4. Moves will be carried out in accordance with the attached March Table.

5. The dividing lines between Brigades will be :-
Between 6th Infantry Brigade and 15th Division-
   (a). In front line - RAILWAY ALLEY - RAILWAY KEEP
                          (to 6th Inf.Brigade).
   (b). In VERMELLES line - Point where GUYS ALLEY cuts
                          LANCASHIRE TRENCH.
   (c). In NOYELLES line - BRAY KEEP (to 6th Inf.Bde.)

Between 6th Inf.Brigade and 5th Inf.Brigade.
   As at present between 2nd and 7th Divisions.

Between 5th Inf.Brigade and 7th Division.
   (a). In front line - ORCHARD STREET (to 5th Inf.Bde.)
   (b). In Village line - PONT FIXE (to 5th Inf.Bde).

6. 2nd Divisional R.A. will assume responsibility for the artillery support of the front to be taken over from the 7th Division under arrangements to be made direct between G.O's C. R.A. concerned, the hour being reported to Divisional H.Q.
   The artillery of the 2nd Division now acting under the orders of the 7th Division will revert to the command of the 2nd Division at the same hour.

7. On the 20th November, one battalion (20th Royal Fusiliers) 98th Inf.Brigade, 33rd Division, will be attached to 19th Inf. Brigade and one battalion (18th Royal Fusiliers) to 6th Inf. Brigade and will commence their training in trench warfare in accordance with separate instructions issued.

8. 2 sections, 5th Field Company, R.E. will remain in Section "Z" and will be affiliated for work to 6th Infantry Brigade.
   2 sections, 11th Field Company, R.E. will be affiliated for work to 5th Infantry Brigade.

9. No.6 Trench Mortar Battery will remain in Section "Z" and will be attached to 6th Infantry Brigade.
   One section No.62 Trench Mortar Battery, now in the trenches with 6th Infantry Brigade will be withdrawn on 23rd instant, and will be attached to 5th Infantry Brigade for work in the trenches. The section No.62 Trench Mortar

Battery

- 2 -

Battery at present billetted with 34th B.A.C. will be at the disposal of 5th Infantry Brigade on 22nd instant.for work in the trenches.

Arrangements for transport will be made direct between 5th Infantry Brigade and R.A., 2nd Division.

10. 2nd Division will take over the evacuation of the new line from 7th Division on 22nd November and will hand over the evacuation of Sub-section Y.4 to 15th Division on 23rd November, under arrangements to be made direct between A.D's.M.S. concerned.

11. The commands of the various sections will be handed over and taken over by Brigade Commanders on completion of the reliefs of the front line and a report forwarded to Divisional Headquarters.

12. Report Centre unchanged.

E Davidson
Captain
for. Major,
General Staff, 2nd Division.

Issued at 24 hrs to :-

```
Copy No.  1..... 5th Infantry Brigade.
    ,,    2..... 6th Infantry Brigade.
    ,,    3..... 19th Infantry Brigade.
    ,,    4..... 98th Infantry Brigade.
    ,,    5..... R.A., 2nd Division.
    ,,    6..... R.E., 2nd Division.
    ,,    7..... Divisional Mounted Troops.
    ,,    8..... No.1 Bty. Motor M G Battery.
    ,,    9..... 2nd Divisional Signal Co.
    ,,   10..... A.D.M.S.
    ,,   11..... A.P.M.
    ,,   12..... "Q".
    ,,   13..... 2nd Divisional Train.
    ,,   14& 14A 1st Corps.              )
    ,,   15..... 15th Division.          )
    ,,   16..... 7th Division.           )
    ,,   17..... 12th Division.          ) For information.
    ,,   18..... 33rd Division.          )
    ,,   19..... 180th Tunnelling Co.R.E.)
    ,,   20..... 251st     ,,       ,,   )
    ,,   21..... 186th Spec. Co. R.E.    )
    ,,   22 - 26. G.S. and record.
```

MARCH TABLE ISSUED WITH 2ND DIVISION OPERATION ORDER No. 75, dated 18th November, 1915.

Date.	Unit.	From.	To.	REMARKS.
20th Nov.	H.Q., 99th Inf.Brigade.	BUSNES Area.	BETHUNE.	
	18th Bn. Royal Fusiliers.	,, ,,	,,	
	20th Bn. Royal Fusiliers.	,, ,,	,,	To join 6th Inf.Brigade.
	1 bn. 6th Inf.Brigade.	BETHUNE.	FOUQUEREUIL.	To join 19th Inf.Brigade.
21st Nov.	3 bns. 6th Inf.Brigade.	(GONNEHEM.	(BEUVRY (N).	) To come under orders of
		(BUSNETTES &	(BETHUNE (Rue D'Aire)	) 19th Infantry Brigade
		(GONNEHEM.	(ANNEQUIN (S).	) till 22nd November
	3 bns. 19th Inf.Brigade.	(BEUVRY (N)	(GONNEHEM.	
		(BETHUNE.(Rue D'Aire)	(BUSNETTES.	
		(ANNEQUIN (S).	(GONNEHEM & BETHUNE.	
	bn. 18th Royal Fusiliers.	BETHUNE.	trenches.	½ battn. to billet 1 night in
	bn. 18th ,, ,,	BETHUNE.	Support.	MONTMORENCY BKS, BETHUNE, with
	bn. 20th ,, ,,	BETHUNE.	trenches.	½ bn. 20th R.Fusiliers.
	bn. 6th Inf. Brigade.	Support.	ANNEQUIN (Fosse).	
22nd Nov.	3 bns. 5th Inf.Brigade.	(BEUVRY (N).	trenches.	
		(ANNEQUIN (S).	trenches.	
	2 bns. 5th Inf.Brigade.	(BETHUNE (Rue D'Aire)	trenches.	
		VENDIN & ANNEZIN.	HARLEY ST. Support	
			Points & BEUVRY (N).	
	1 bn. 20th Royal Fusiliers.	Trenches.	ANNEQUIN (S).	
	bn. ,, ,, ,,	BETHUNE.	trenches.	
	bn. 18th ,, ,,	BETHUNE.	Support.	
	bn. 18th ,, ,,	Trenches.	trenches.	
	1 bn. 3rd Inf.Bde.	Support.	ANNEQUIN (Fosse).	
	½ ,,	FOUQUEREUIL.		Come under orders of 12th Div. till 24th.
	bn. 19th Inf. Bde.	BETHUNE.	GONNEHEM.	1 bn. 6th Bde.at ANNEQUIN (N) under orders 19th Bde.till 23rd. 1 bn. 7th Div.at LE PREOL will also be under orders 19th Bde. till 23rd.

MARCH TABLE (Continued).

Date.	Unit.	From.	To.	Remarks.
23rd Nov.	2 bns. 19th Inf. Brigade.	Trenches.	VENDIN & ANNEZIN.	
	2 bns. 6th Inf. Brigade.	(Support & ANNEQUIN (Fosse). (ANNEQUIN (N).	Trenches ("Z" Sect.)	
	1 bn. 6th Inf. Brigade.	Trenches.	SAILLY LABOURSE.	Under orders of 12th Div.
	18th Royal Fusiliers.	Trenches & ANNEQUIN (Fosse).	ANNEQUIN (S).	Will come under orders of 5th Infantry Brigade.
	20th Royal Fusiliers.	Trenches & ANNEQUIN (S).	ANNEQUIN (N)	
24th Nov.	1 bn. 6th Inf. Brigade.	SAILLY LABOURSE.	BETHUNE (Rue D'Aire)	To be clear of SAILLY LABOURSE by noon.

DAILY DIARY.

Z group.   22-11-15

9th Bntt. Retaliated on German support
trenches and on AUCHY.
8th Batt. fired on Russian point in
retaliation to MINEN WERFER
and on Auchy Checked registration
on Madagascar.
17th Batt. fired on German parapet
immediately after 'Mine' went
up at 6.15am
48th Batt. fired on AUCHY and
HAINES
17 How Batt. fired one time
on FRANKs keep and Ascot to stop
Munenwerfer. Also twice on
A22c06 and A21c87. at request
of infantry.
We blew up and occupied mine
crater at 6.15 am today.
Very foggy all day observation
impossible.

                    [signed]
                 Adj. 41. Bde.

A
2ND DIV

There is nothing to note for
to-days diary
All Batteries report very quiet
on the front and owing to the
Fog they have not fired since
yesterday evening
The enemy fired a few 77 m m
shell on A1 2ND line trenches
but it was impossible to tell
from which direction time 10 A.M.
The relief was completed to-day
and the Infantry Battalions visited

22/11/15

B Quiller Couch
Lieut & Adj
for O.C. A Group

2nd DIVISION
GENERAL STAFF
No. GS 712/2
Date 18/11/15

R.A. 2nd Division

With reference to 1st Corps No. G.153. of 17th inst. forwarded to you under my No. G.S. 712/1 of 18th inst.

Please note that under para 3. Artillery relief will take place on nights 21st/22nd and 22nd/23rd inst. and not as stated therein.

———

E. Davidson
Captain
S.

2 Div.
18/11/15

SECRET

COPY NO. 12.

2nd DIVISION ARTILLERY OPERATION ORDER NO. 7.

Reference BETHUNE Combined Sheet 1/40,000.

19th Novr, 1915.

1. On 22nd November, 5th Infantry Brigade takes over the front from GUN STREET (A.21.d.4.9.) to WILLOW ROAD (A.9.d.4.4.) from 7th Division.

2. On 23rd November, 6th Infantry Brigade will hand over the front from SAVILE ROW to MUD TRENCH (A.22.c.6.1) to 48th Infantry Brigade (15th Division), and will take over the front from R.1 to GUN STREET, from 19th Infantry Brigade.

3. 2nd Division Artillery will assume responsibility for the support of the front up to WILLOW ROAD at the same hour as the infantry relief on the 22nd, (when the 34th Brigade will return to command of 2nd Division), and will hand over responsibility for the front SAVILE ROW to MUD STREET on the 24th at the same hour as that front is taken over by the 15th Division.

4. 71st Battery will relieve 12th Battery, 7th Division on the 21st/22nd and 22nd/23rd with 4 guns (to come under 34th Brigade); and A/62 Battery, 12th Division on 21st/22nd with 2 guns (to come under 41st Brigade).
Guns will be taken over on relief.

5. 41st Brigade will assume responsibility for the front from MUD STREET to R.1 (in addition to their present front) on the 23rd at the same hour as the 6th Brigade takes over up to GUN STREET.

6. 64th Brigade will withdraw from action on 23rd/24th and 24th/25th and will return to 12th Division command.
Responsibility for the front MUD STREET to R.1 will be handed over to 41st Brigade on 23rd, and for SAVILE ROW to MUD STREET to the 71st Brigade, 15th Division Artillery on the 24th, at the same hours as the infantry reliefs.

Major, R.A.,

Brigade Major, R.A., 2nd Divn.

Issued at .... to :-

Copy No. 1. 34th Brigade.
" " 2. 36th "
" " 3. 41st "
" " 4. 44th "
" " 5. D.A.C.
" " 6. 2nd Division G.S.)
" " 7. 7th Divn. Artillery.)
" " 8. 12th Divn. Artillery.) For information.
" " 9. 15th Divn. Artillery.)

2nd Division Artillery Summary.

19th November, 1915.

Position of guns located.

    N I L.

Flashes.

    N I L.

Hostile Artillery Fire.

No.	Time.	Nature.	Target.	From. direction of	Remarks.
1.	6-7 a	77 m.m.	G.4.d.0.5.	Dump.	7 Rounds.
2.	9.8 a	77 m.m.	A.27.b.1.5.	unknown.	
3.	10.10 a	77 m.m.	A.27.c.2.2.	"	
4.	11.30 a	77 m.m.	G.4.d.0.5.	Dump.	8 Rounds.
5.	1.0 p	77 m.m.	Railway G.3.b.	do	5 Rounds.
6.	1.10 p	4.2 How.	A.27.b.2.7.	Haisnes.	11 Rounds.
7.	1.15 p	?	Sim's Koop.	unknown.	Light gun.
8.	1.50 p	5.9 How.	A.27.d.4.3.	Auchy.	11 rounds (10 blind)
9.	2.45 to 3.10p	77 m.m.	Mine Point trenches.	unknown.	
10.	4.0 p	105 m.m.	Vermelles.	unknown.	
11.		105 m.m.	Ponte Fixe.	unknown.	
12.		77 m.m.	Z.1.trenches	unknown.	
13.	3.30 to 4.0 p	15 c.m.	Canal.	unknown.	6
14.	"	77 m.m.	do	unknown.	20
15.	4.10 p	77 m.m.	Trenches Y.	Triangle.	

Action by our artillery.

    Wire cut in A.27.b. between 7.9 and 9.7 and at Mad Point Other fire in retaliation.

General.

    It is reported that H.E. fire on HAISNES seems to stop shelling of Quarry and of Annequin.

    Major, R.A.,

Brigade Major, R.A., 2nd Divn.

"A" Form.   Army Form C. 2121.

MESSAGES AND SIGNALS.   No. of Message _____

Prefix ___ Code ___ m.	Words	Charge	This message is on a/c of:	Recd. at 1.15 m.
Office of Origin and Service Instructions.	Sent			Date _____
Secret	At ___ m.		___ Service.	From _____
	To ___			
	By ___		(Signature of "Franking Officer")	By _____

TO   2nd Div G

* Sender's Number	Day of Month	In reply to Number	AAA
BM 902	19		

Organization of artillery for new
front will be

A Group   7 1" Battery (4)   A18a88
            50   "   F18a3.2
            70   "   F24c9.2
            7 mm   (2)   AN25.2
            56   "   A20a5.2

Z Group   9   "   F15c3.1
            17   "   F24a8.8
            18   "   A19d.1.1
            15   "   L8a0.5
            7 1"   "   (2)   A14c26
            4 7"   "   F30c6.2

Z covers from La Bassée Road to gun shell fr A.

From
Place   R A 7 Div
Time   10.30 am

The above may be forwarded as now corrected.   (Z)

Censor.   Signature of Addressor or person authorised to telegraph in his name
* This line should be erased if not required.

1489

DAILY AMMUNITION RETURN

DATE 19th Nov. 1915

BATTERIES.

Piece	Projectile	Code	50	70	15	48	71	9	16	17	47	56	Total	Per Piece
18-pr	Guns.......													
	Shrapnel...	"A"	67	10	15	97	–	44	–	33	–	–	266	
	H. E.......	"Ax"	–	6	4	30	–	98	–	13	–	–	151	
4.5"	Howitzers..		–	–	–	–	–	–	–	–	–	–	–	
	Shrapnel...	"B"	–	–	–	–	–	–	–	–	–	2	2	
	H. E.......	"Bx"	–	–	–	–	–	–	–	–	–	–	–	

2nd Division Artillery Orders

by

Brigadier-General G.H. SANDERS, D.S.O., Comdg R.A. 2nd Divn.

19th November, 1915.

1121. R.A. ORDERS.

Were not issued yesterday, 18th November, 1915.

1122. POSTING.

Captain E.G.L. CULLUM from Adjutant D.A.C., to 41st Brigade, R.F.A., with effect from 18th November.

1123. COURTMARTIAL.

A F.G.C.M., will assemble at 44th B.A.C. Headquarters (RUE GAMBETTA BETHUNE) at 10-0 a.m. on Monday, 21st Novr, '15 for the trial of No. 88586 Fitter Staff Sergeant A. McEachran, 36th Brigade, R.F.A., Headquarters, and No. 7259, Sergeant A. Vaughan, A.V.C., attached 23rd Heavy Battery, R.G.A., and such other accused persons as may be brought before it :-

PRESIDENT.
Major H.H. Joll.   -   17th Battery, R.F.A.

MEMBERS.
Captain W.E. Maitland Dougall, - 50th Battery, R.F.A.
Lieutenant T.J. Moss.   - 70th Battery, R.F.A.

The accused will be warned and all witnesses duly required to attend.
Proceedings to be sent to Staff Captain, R.A., 2nd Division.
The 36th Brigade will detail the Court Orderly and supply the necessary stationery.

L.G. BUXTON, Capt, R.A.,
Staff Captain, R.A., 2nd Division.

SECRET.

2nd Division No. G.S.740.

2nd Division.

No. 1/C.A./22.   19th Nov.'15.
----

1. The 81st Siege Battery will move from its present position at F.18.c.8.6. to a new position at F.5.a.7.3 on the nights 24th/25th and 25th/26th November, 1915.

2. For tactical purposes the 81st Siege Battery will be placed under the orders of the G.O.C. Northern Division of the 1st Corps from the time that its sections arrive in the new position.

The 59th Siege Battery at F.30.c.8.6 will similarly be placed under the orders of the G.O.C. Southern Division of the 1st Corps from 6 a.m. on 25th November, 1915.

3. One section 22nd Heavy Battery will join its Headquarters section at LOISNE when the billets are vacated and the 21st Heavy Battery will move to its new position in A.25 as soon as the pits are ready.

(Sgd) Noel Birch   Brig-General.
for B.G.G.S. 1st Corps.

2.

"Q" 2nd Division.
R.A., 2nd Division.

59th Siege Battery will be under the orders of G.O.C. R.A., 2nd Division, from 6 a.m. 25th November, 1915.

2nd Division.
21. 11. 1915.

Belgrave   Major.
General Staff, 2nd Division.

Report on Wirecutting 2nd Div.
Week Ending 20/11/15

No	Position	Extent	Rounds fired	Remarks
1	A 28 d 1½ ½	30ˣ	180	Mostly old coils. Little effect.
2	A 28 c 9 4	30ˣ	90	High new wire on stakes. All considerably damaged.
3	MAD POINT	40ˣ	150	Very thick old coils. Effect fair.
4	A 28 a d 1½	30ˣ	90	Supdd. ~~~~~~ Low wire. Effect good.
5	A 27 67·9 – 9·7	130ˣ	454	All considerably damaged. Clear gap of 5ˣ. Little effect on parapets in all cases.

C R A 2nd Divn

2nd Division Artillery Summary.

20th November, 1915.
****

Position of guns located.

A.23.c.5.6½ - Field guns. These guns were engaged at 4 p.m. by 9th Battery and by the whole group at 5 p.m. They ceased fire in each case.

Flashes seen.

Heavy howitzer battery firing towards VERMELLES at 4-15p.m 108 magnetic from Wilson's House.
Heavy howitzer firing towards VERMELLES at 5 p.m. 105½ true from Braddell Castle.

Hostile Artillery fire

No.	Time from	to	Nature	Target.	From direction of	Remarks.
1.	11a	3-0p	15 c.m.	PONT FIXE	?	
2.	11-30a,	12-30 p	4.2 or 5.9	do.	?	30 Rounds
3.	11-30 a		)			Ceased when
	11-45 a		) 10.5 c.m.	QUARRY.	Haisnes.	heavies
	12-30 p		)			shelled
	1-15 p		)			Haisnes.
4.	1-5 p		10.5 c.m.	CAMBRIN.	Auchy.	4 Rounds.
5.	1-55 p		77 m.m.	A.21.b.2.2.	?	14 Rounds.
6.	3-0 p		77 m.m.	CURRAGH GRANGE	?	
7.	2-40 p		77 m.m.	BRADDELL 1st	Auchy.	5 Rounds.
8.	3-0 p.m.		77 m.m.	EURBURE.	Auchy.	10 Rounds.
9.	3-0 p		77 m.m.	MINE Pt.	Auchy.	2 Rounds.
10.	3-45 p		77 m.m.	A.21.b.2.6.	Auchy.	10 Rounds.
11.	2pm	5pm	(77 m.m. (15 c.m.	Railway position A.27.d. Central & Right Boyau	?	continuous bombardment
12.	3-0 p		77 m.m.	HUMANITY.	Auchy ?	

Action by our Artillery.

Z Group retaliated for numbers 5,7,8,9 & 10, A.25.c.5.6½ was thought to be the source of all the Auchy fire.
Working parties dispersed - Cemetery Alley. A.29.a.7.5. and Plumtree House. Other fire in retaliation.

[P.T.O

New Work.

Considerable amount of work in second line, especially near Frank's Koop.

Mounds of earth covered with white chalk have taken the place of haystack near A.22.d.8.5.

Enemy is digging a communication trench about A.29.a.7.5.

General.

A cross erected by the enemy on the South of the Canal bears the following :-

For King and Fatherland. Died like heroes. Captain Kilby Captain Williams and 13 men of South Staffs. Regt. German follows.

                                            Major, R.A.,

                          Brigade Major, R.A., 2nd Divn.

1492

DAILY AMMUNITION RETURN

DATE 20 Nov 1915

BATTERIES.

Piece	Projectile	Code	50	70	15	48	71	9	16	17	47	56	Total Per Piece
18-pr	Guns......												
	Shrapnel...	"A"	53	14	80	558	–	86	14	38	–	–	843
	H.E.......	"Ax"	80	26	–	96	–	86	–	100	–	–	388
4.5"	Howitzers..												
	Shrapnel...	"B"									–	–	–
	H.E.......	"Bx"									4	90	94

2nd Division Artillery Orders

by

Brigadier-General G.H.SANDERS, D.S.O., Comdg.R.A., 2nd Divn.

20th November, 1915.

1124. COURTMARTIAL.

With reference to D.A.Order No.1123 of yesterday, the Court therein referred to will assemble at Headquarters, 2nd Division Artillery, (18 RUE SADI CARNOT, BETHUNE) on Monday, 22nd November, instead of at Headquarters, 44th B.A.C.

1125. SMOKE HELMETS FOR HORSES.

O's.C.Units should inform A.D.V.S. direct whether they have any deficiencies in smoke helmets for horses, and whether any of those smoke helmets in hand require re-dipping.

1126. PROMOTIONS.

O's.C.Units should send in names of officers holding Temporary Commissions who are recommended for promotion by 8 p.m. on 22nd inst.

1127. DIVINE SERVICE.

Divine Service will be held at 9-30 a.m. for all units in BETHUNE, in Rue d'Aire Chapel.
It is important that as many men as possible should attend this Service.
A Service for Roman Catholics will be held at BETHUNE CATHEDRAL at 10-30 a.m. Service for Wesleyans and Free Church at 9-0 a.m. in Recreation Room, Rue d'Arras, and Voluntary Service at 6-0 p.m. in Recreation Room, Rue d'Aire.

L.G.BUXTON, Capt, R.A.

Staff Captain, R.A., 2nd Divn.

SECRET

COPY NO. R. 12.

2nd DIVISION ARTILLERY OPERATION ORDER NO.7.
AMENDMENT.

20th November, 1915.

For para.2.read -

On 23rd November 6th Infantry Brigade takes over the front from R.1. to GUN STREET from 19th Infantry Bde., and one battalion 48th Infantry Brigade, 15th Division, comes under the orders of 6th Infantry Brigade in the section SAVILE ROW to MUD TRENCH A.28.c.6.1.

On 24th November 6th Infantry Brigade hands over the front from SAVILE ROW to MUD TRENCH to 48th Brigade.

(signature)
Major, R.A.,
Brigade Major, R.A., 2nd Division.

Issued at 2.30/m to :-

Copy No. 1.	34th Brigade.
" " 2.	36th "
" " 3.	41st "
" " 4.	44th "
" " 5.	D.A.C.
" " 6.	2nd Division G.S.)
" " 7.	7th Divn. Artillery.) For information.
" " 8.	12th " ")
" " 9.	15th " ")

2nd Division Artillery Summary.

21st November, 1915.

Positions of guns located.

N I L.

Flashes.
4-10 p.m. 20th, 77 m.m. gun firing rapidly at 103° magnetic from A.26.b.2.9¼.
4-0 p.m. 21st, howitzer (?) firing rapidly at 107½° magnetic from A.26.b.2.9¼.

Hostile Artillery Fire.

No.	Time.	Nature.	Target.	From direction of	Remarks.
1.	10-0 a	77 m.m.) 105 m.m.) 150 m.m.)	Railway. A.27.d.7.5. Barts.	Haisnes.	ceased on retaliation on Corons Alley.
2.	10.25-10.50	77 m.m.	A.27.a.5.0.	Auchy.	20 Rounds.
3.	10.30-11.0.	77 m.m.	Vermelles-Auchy Road.	Auchy.	5 Rounds.
4.	10.30-10.50	4.2 how.	A.27.d. trenches.	?	8 Rounds.
5.	11 10 a	77 m.m.	Cambrin Church.	Auchy.	1 Round.
6.	12.45 p	15 c.m.	A.27.a.9.8.	Haisnes.	
7.	12.50 p	4.2 how.	A.27.a.4.5.	?	4 Rounds H.E.
8.	1.13 -1.20p	5.9 how.) 4.2 how.)	A.21.d.1.9.	?	1 Round each.
9.	2-0 p	77 m.m.	Mine point.	Auchy.	10 Rounds.
10.	2.15-2.30 p	77 m.m.	Z.2.trenches.	?	6 Rounds.
11.	2.15-2.30 p	105m.m.	Vermelles-Auchy Road	?	8 Rounds.
12.	3-0 p	(105m.m.) (77 m.m.)	Quarry.	Haisnes.	8 Rounds at short interval.
13.	3.15-3.18 p	150 m.m.	Trenches.Z.1.	?	2 Rounds.

Action by our Artillery.
Z Group retaliated on Auchy, Les Briques, Mine Point, Lean-to Cottage and Railway for 5,6,10 & 13. Y Group retaliated on Corons Alley and Les Briques, for shelling of Barts.
Other fire to stop work at night and to silence Minenwerfers.
Last night (20th) Y Group retaliated on Haisnes Cross Roads, Fosse Trench and Corons Alley, for heavy shelling of Y trenches.

Work done.
Enemy has been repairing wire along trench S.E. of Mad Point. Some fresh work at Frank's Keep.

Working parties dispersed.
A.29.a.4.7.

Mowbray
Major, R.A.,
Brigade Major, R.A., 2nd Divn.

1495

DAILY AMMUNITION RETURN

DATE 21. XI. 15.

BATTERIES.

Piece	Projectile	Code	50	70	15	48	71	9	16	17	47	56	Total	Per Piece
18-pr	Guns.......													
	Shrapnel...	"A"	37	48	32	62	-	98	41	74	-	-	392	
	H. E.......	"Ax"	45	90	4	2	-	77	-	75	-	-	293	
4.5"	Howitzers..													
	Shrapnel...	"B"									-	-	-	
	H. E.......	"Bx"									39	39	78	

2nd Division Artillery Orders

by

Brigadier-General G.H.SANDERS, D.S.O., Comdg.R.A., 2nd Divn.

21st November, 1915.

1128. PERISCOPES.

All units who have received the No.19 or No.5 Periscope should re-submit demands for No.14. and endorse the Indent "when supply becomes available, to replace No. 19 or No.5 received".

1129. POSTING.

2nd Lieutenant R.G.THOMAS from 47th Battery, 44th Brigade to 36th Brigade. O.C. 36th Brigade will please report date of joining in due course.

L.G.BUXTON, Capt, R.A.,

Staff Captain, R.A., 2nd Divn.

"A" Form. Army Form C. 2121.

MESSAGES AND SIGNALS. No. of Message_____

Prefix____ Code____ m. Office of Origin and Service Instructions.	Words	Charge	This message is on a/c of: _____Service.	Recd. at____m. Date From By____
	Sent At____m. To____ By____		(Signature of "Franking Officer")	

TO 2ⁿᵈ Divⁿ G

Sender's Number Bm 909	Day of Month 21	In reply to Number	AAA

2ⁿᵈ Divⁿ Artillery CO J para 6 —— 13ᵗʰ Division Artillery arrive to-night their battery on to our front SAVILE ROW to MILD TRENCH a day earlier ie on 22/23 and 23/24 71ˢᵗ Brigade taking over trenches held by 6.4ᵗʰ on 23ʳᵈ at same time as infantry responsibility changes our 7ᵗʰ Brigade HQ will go into house occupied by 6.4ᵗʰ and will therefore be moved to us and we see no objection and 1st Corps agree RA have none 71ˢᵗ Brigade will be under 2nd Div orders until 24ᵗʰ when that front is handed over to 13ᵗʰ Division

From RA 1 Div
Place
Time 5.15 pm

The above may be forwarded as now corrected. (Z) Minkey Major
Censor. Signature of Addresser or person authorised to telegraph in his name
* This line should be erased if not required.

64th Brigade RFA Nov 21/22 - 1915

Time	No of rounds	Reported by	Nature of Guns	Target	Notes
6.20 p.m	90	OC D/64	18 pdr.	Transport in rear of DUMP.	
12.30 p.m	6	OC B/64	"	A.22.d.2.1.	To silence enfilade fire

General Information.

Machine gun reported. Mag Bearing 12° from A.28.c.2.6½.

P Barton
Lt Col RFA.
Comdg. 64th Bde RFA

"A" Form. Army Form C. 2121.

MESSAGES AND SIGNALS.

Prefix	Code	m.	Words	Charge	This message is on a/c of:	Recd. at	m.
Office of Origin and Service Instructions.			Sent			Date	
			At	m.	Service.	From	
			To			By	
			By		(Signature of "Franking Officer")		

TO { HA 1st Corps   7 DA   12 DA

Sender's Number	Day of Month	In reply to Number	
Bm 914	22		AAA

Action by enemys artillery

aaa NIL aaa

From: Ka Wn
Place:
Time: 6 10 pm

The above may be forwarded as now corrected. (Z)

Censor. Signature of Addressor or person authorised to telegraph in his name

2nd Division Artillery.

Winter Training.

2nd Divisional Artillery
No. B.M. 1/2 36
Date 22.11.15

1. Brigade Commanders will ensure that all young officers have a good working knowledge of the following subjects :-

   (a). Military law both as regards Court Martial and the powers of a C.O.

   (b). Interior economy of a battery, system of paying, obtaining supplies, clothing, etc.

   (c). Horse management, including shoeing and fitting, and care of horses.

2. Officers, N.C.O's and gunners of B.A.C's should be brought up in turn to do a short course with the batteries in action. If necessary they may be temporarily replaced by men from the batteries. When this has been completed arrangements will be made for N.C.O's and gunners from the D.A.C. to do the same.

3. An ample reserve of telephonists must be formed either by training extra men in the batteries or forming Brigade classes as most convenient.

When men have reached a certain standard, application should be made for them to attend the Divisional Signal School.

4. A proportion of drivers should learn the simpler duties of the guns.

                                                      Monkary Major

                                          Brigade Major, ~~Brigadier-General,~~

R.A., 2nd Divn.
22-11-1915.   ~~Cmdg.~~ R.A., 2nd Division.

Copies to :-
   34th Brigade, R.F.A.
   36th   "   "
   41st   "   "
   44th   "   "
   D.A.C.

2nd Division Artillery Orders

by

Brigadier-General G.H.SANDERS, D.S.O., Comdg.R.A.,2nd Divn.

22nd November,1915.

1130. COURTMARTIAL.

The F.G.C.M., of which Major H.H.JOLL, 17th Battery is President will re-assemble at the 50th Battery Wagon lines (F 13 c 9 9), at noon to-morrow,Tuesday 23rd November,1915, to consider a matter to be laid before it.

1131. UNDERCLOTHING.

It has been decided that the scale of issue of drawers for mounted men laid down in G.R.O.1201 will be adhered to.

L.G.BUXTON, Capt, R.A.,

Staff Captain, R.A., 2nd Division.

DAILY DIARY 1564

Z group.   23-11-15

9th Batt. nothing to report.
15th Batt. fired several times on
POPES nose and vicinity at request
of infantry. Madagaskar trench
and Madagascar registration
checked.
17th Batt nothing to report.
47th Batt. fired 10 times 60 rds on
A22c0.6. and A21c8.7. at request
of infantry.
48th Batt fired on gap in wire
and on AVCUY because it was foggy
also on railway to.

Third sect 48th registered from new
position.

    Very foggy all day.

                Rodd
                41st Bde

BRIGADE R.F.A. DAILY REPORT.

DATE. Nov 23rd 1915

POSITION OF GUNS LOCATED. NIL

FLASHES. NIL

HOSTILE ARTILLERY FIRE

No.	Time	Nature	Target	From direction of	Remarks,
1	4.20 PM	77 mm	HOLLOW	—	Too misty to locate direction
2	1 PM	Small MINEN-WERFER	A 2	K Brickstack.	

ACTION BY OUR ARTILLERY.

GENERAL.

50TH Battery fired at 5.30 AM on the gap they cut in wire A 16 C ½ . 4 ¾
At 11.30 AM fire on working party reported by Infantry on Embankment redoubt.

56 Battery 6 PM fired on working party at NE Brickstack at request of Infantry
1 PM fired on "K" Brickstack in retaliation for MINNENWERFER and Trench Bombs fired on our trenches in A 2.
2.35 PM fired on working party on RAILWAY EMBANKMENT.

70TH Battery Observation possible only between 1 and 2 PM. Fired a few rounds at WORKING PARTY A 21 C 8.8

71ST Battery Fired 60 rounds registering trenches from CANAL to Pt 82
And 40 rounds on A17a & A17c

Commanding Brigade R.F.A.

Brigade Major
R.A. 2nd Divn.

A Group

36 BRIGADE R.F.A. DAILY REPORT.

DATE. Nov. 23. 1915

POSITION OF GUNS LOCATED. NIL

FLASHES. NIL

HOSTILE ARTILLERY FIRE

No.	Time	Nature	Target	From direction of	Remarks
1	4.20 PM	77 mm	THE HOLLOW	—	Too Misty to see
2	1 PM	Small MINNENWERFER	A2 Trenches	"K" BRICKSTACK	56 HOWS retaliated

ACTION BY OUR ARTILLERY.

50TH Battery fired on the gap they cut in Enemy's wire on 21/11/15 A 16 C ½ . 5 at 5.30 AM and 12.30 PM. Also fired on Working party reported by Infantry on Embankment at 11.30 AM

GENERAL.

56TH Battery Fired on working party near NE Brickstack at 6 PM reported by Infantry. 1 PM fired on K Brickstack in retaliation for MINNIE and Bombs. 2.35 fired on working party on Embankment.

70TH Battery Dispersed small working party at A 21 G 8 8 at 1.40 PM

71ST Battery Registered trenches from CANAL to Pt 82 and A 17 a and C
The light was too bad for close observation But trenches could be seen fairly clearly 1 PM to 2 PM

B. Quiller Couch
Lieut & Adj
for Commanding 36 Brigade R.F.A.

A Group.

Brigade Major
R.A. 2nd Divn.

2nd Division Artillery Report.

23rd November, 1915.

General.

47th Howitzer Battery fired on A.22.c.0.6 and A.21.c.8.7. in answer to 2.

Nothing visible.

Hostile Artillery Fire.

Time. From	Time. To	Nature.	Direction from.	Target.	Remarks.
1. 11-0a.m.		77 m.m.	Auchy.	Crater.	4 Rds. Percussion
2. 12-30p.m		77 m.m.	Auchy.	Mine Point Trenches.	6 Rounds.
3. 12-30pm	1-0 pm	105 m.m.	Auchy.	Russels Keep.	6 Rounds.
4. 2-30pm		?	Auchy.	?	Passed over Cambrin, no burst being heard.

Major, R.A.,

Brigade Major, R.A., 2nd Divn.

"A" Form.
Army Form C. 2121.

MESSAGES AND SIGNALS.

No. of Message **1505**

Prefix	Code	m.	Words	Charge	This message is on a/c of:	Recd. at m.
Office of Origin and Service Instructions.			Sent At m.		Service.	Date
			To			From
			By		(Signature of "Franking Officer.")	By

TO — **2ND D.A**

Sender's Number	Day of Month	In reply to Number	AAA
C 39	23		

The 71st Bde have relieved 64th Bde

From — **OC 64 Bde**
Place —
Time — **5.35 pm**

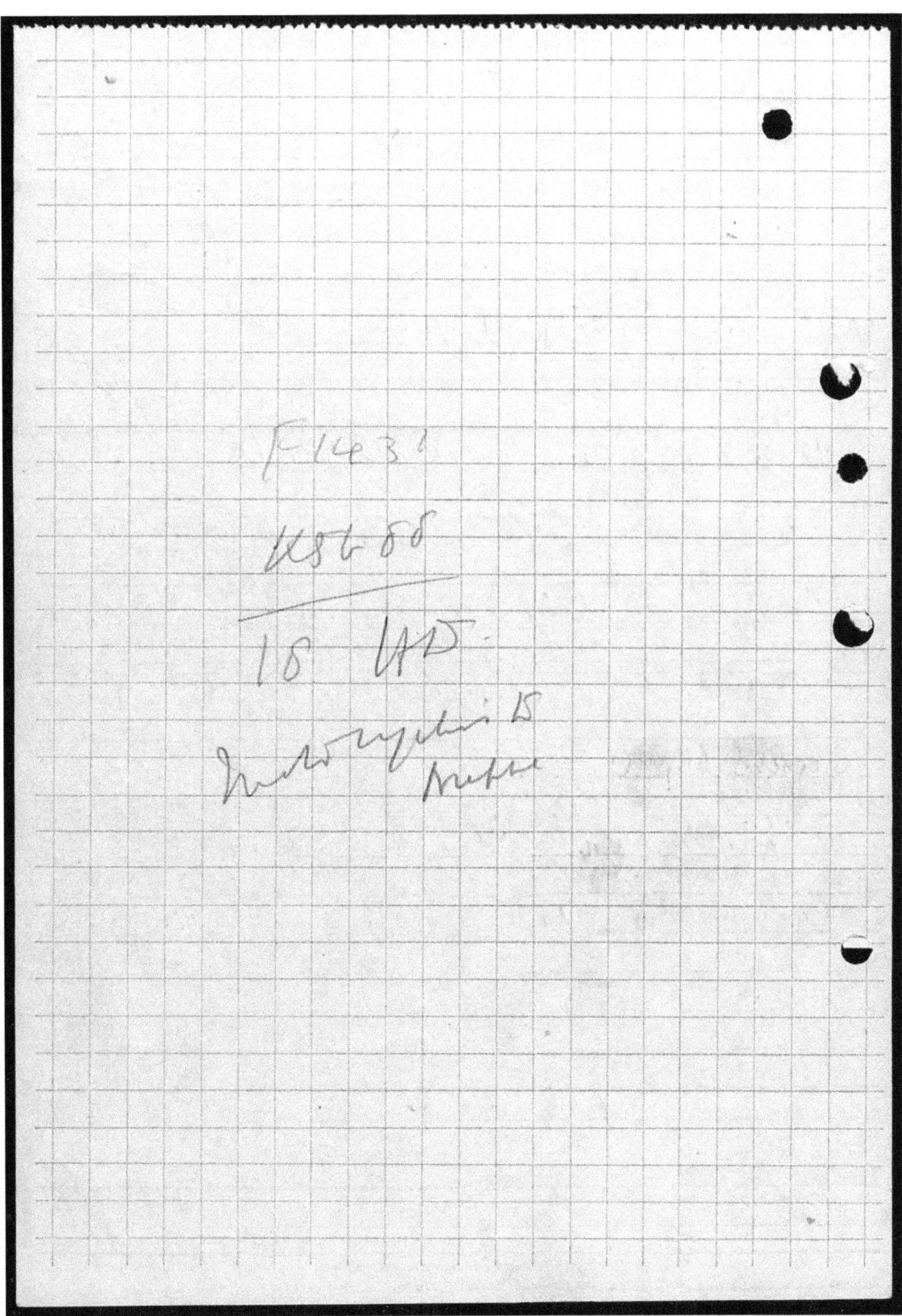

1506

DAILY AMMUNITION RETURN

DATE 23.XI.15

BATTERIES.

Piece	Projectile	Code	50	70	15	48	71	9	16	17	47	56	Total	Per Piece
18-pr	Guns......													
	Shrapnel...	"A"	18	-	57	60	60	6	-	105	-	-	306	
	H.E......	"Ax"	-	-	6	25	-	26	-	22	-	-	79	
4.5"	Howitzers..													
	Shrapnel...	"B"									-	-	-	
	H.E.......	"Bx"									113	3	116	

2nd Division Artillery Orders

by

Brigadier-General G.H. SANDERS, D.S.O., Comdg. R.A., 2nd Divn.

23rd November, 1915.

1132. REST HOUSE.

The present Rest House for men going and coming off leave is required for a billet. Another house has been taken viz:- No: 10 BOULEVARD THIERS opposite the open air swimming bath and will be brought into use on the night of the 24th:

1133. BLANKETS - ISSUE OF SECOND,

The issue of a second blanket per man for all troops in the field during the winter months has now been approved subject to the condition that Divisional Commanders shall arrange for their collection and storage in case of a move.
Indents should be sent to Ordnance Officers concerned and issue will be made as supplies become available.
(Authority - G.R.O. No:1270 d/21-11-1915).

1134. CASUALTY RETURNS.

Casualty returns must be rendered punctually at 9-30 a.m. each day.
"Nil" returns must be rendered when there are no casualties to report.

L.G. BUXTON, Capt, R.A.,

Staff Captain, R.A., 2nd Divn.

2nd D.A.

GROUP DIARY.

B.

DATE -

General. Light good. Observation possible 8 am
Enemy's artillery active.
Lamp signalling picked up 1.50 pm fr DOUVRIN.
Smoke seen issuing from ruined house in rear of
DIAMOND DOOR COTTAGE.
Mine blown up in Z2. Our parapet & front trench
blown in. 9 & 17 Batteries opened fire while working party at.

Enemy's Works.

Embankment Redoubt - new work.
Between A & B brickstacks - new earth.
A 22 d 3.4 - new earth

Flashes seen 110° fr Braddell Castle. Time of flight
8 seconds.

	Action. Time.					
No.	From.	To.	Battery.	Target.	Rounds.	Remarks.

Lieut.Colonel.
Commanding Group.

Action.

No.	Time. From.	To.	Battery.	Target.	Rounds.	Remarks.
(1)	11.15 AM	12 noon	M^{TN} BTY	BRICK STACK TRENCH & A 21 b 9.9	18	
(2)	9.45 PM		50TH	EMBANKMENT	6	WORKING PARTY
(3)	11 AM		50TH	ENEMY'S 2ND LINE	9	Retaliation for MINNIES
(4)	3.50 PM		50TH	" " "	17	Retaliation
(5)	4.30 PM	9 PM	56TH	K BRICKSTACK	19	MINNIES ACTIVE
(6)	9.40 AM	9.45 AM	56	A 11 d 7.9 & A 11 a 5.7 Enemy in open	12	MATERIAL abandoned in rush for cover
(7)	10.30 AM		56	MINNENWERFER	7	Request of HLI
(8)	11.25 AM		56	"	7	Has not fired once.
(9)	12.5 PM		56	ENEMY working between A & B Brickstack	6	Retaliation
(10)	1.45 PM		56	EMBANKMENT REDOUBT	5	Reply to Rifle grenades
(11)	2.26 PM		56	NE Brickstack	5	
12	9.40	10 PM	70	ENEMYS TRENCHES N of MAIN ROAD	12	Retaliation
13	10.30 AM		70	"	15	"
14	1 PM	3.50	70	"	32	"
15	7.45 PM		71	ROAD A 16 B 4.0	12	Transport heard
16	8.30 PM		71	" A 16 d 9.0	14	"
17	9.30 AM		71	A 18 d Working Party	18	Dispersed
18	2.30 PM	3 PM	71	ENEMY'S TRENCHES N of CANAL	25	Retaliation

B. Quiller Couch.
Lieut & Adj
for
Lieut. Colonel.
Commanding A Group.

No.	Time From.	Time To.	Battery.	Target.	Rounds.	Remarks.
	9.30 am		17th Battery	German trenches grenades		to stop rifle
	10.30 am	11. am		Emplacement opposite		Began 19 as reported
	11.40 am			HAINES to retaliate for shell on Braddell point		
	1.30 pm			as above for shell on Cambrin		
	1.50 pm			a few rounds into Auchy		
	4.20 pm	4.45 pm		German trenches down after mine went up		to keep germans
	10.43 am		47th Batt.	FRANKS keep & A 22 C 06.	14	retaliation to MINNIE
	3.49 pm			" "	4	"
	4.26 pm			" "	8	at request of infantry
	10.30 am		9th	trench S of road at request of infantry		to silence Minenwerfer
	12.15 pm			hostile gun in A 29 c 29		
	1.30 pm	2 pm		Shelled Auchy		
	3.15 pm			New german craters		at request of inf.
	4.20 pm	4.45 pm		german trenches		To keep germans down

Retaliated three or four times to hostile fire; on german trenches; comm. trenches; and Auchy.

			15th Battery			
	4.5 am 10.30 am		12 rds	Madagascar t.		at request of Suffolks
	12.30 pm	1.45 pm	49 rds	Madagascar t. Auchy alley Lone farm		retaliation and registration checked
	3.20 pm		6 rds	Mad Alley Auchy alley		registration
	3.30 pm	4.30		Tram alley		registration 3 rds
	3.50 pm			Cottage A 28 b 5.1	10 rds	zero line for new gun

Also retaliated on Auchy for hostile fire

			48th Batt.			
	7.50 pm			AUCHY	16	Transport reported there
	8.10 pm			HAINES with HE		
	7 am			Railway trench	6	
	7.50 am			Washing party LONE farm		dispersed
	9 am			fired on Auchy and railway to		in retaliation
	12.45 am	12.10 pm				

Registration of 712th Det Sect. was completed.

2nd Division Hostile Fire Report.

24th November-1915.

1. <u>General Information.</u>

N I L,

2. Hostile Fire.

No.	Time. From.	To.	Nature.	Direction from.	Area shelled.	Remarks
1.	9-10 a	9-15 a	77 m.m.	Auchy.	Z1 Comm.Trench	A few.
2.	10-5 a	10-20 a	77 m.m.	,,	A 21 d 1 9	14 Rounds.
3.	11-15 a	11-30 a	105 m.m.	,,	A 20 b 3 9	6 Rounds.*
4.	11-20 a	12-0	105 m.m.	?	Harley St.	
5.	11-25 a	11-50 a	150 m.m.	Auchy.	Sunken Road.	
6.	11-30 a	11-50 a	105 m.m.	,,	A 20 a 9 3	1 Round.
7.	11-30 a	12-10 p	105 m.m.	,,	A 19 b	6 Rounds.*
8.	12-0		77 m.m.	La Bassee.	Cambrin.	2 Rounds.*
9.	12-55 p	1-5 p	105 m.m.	Douvrin.	Givenchy.	
10.	1-25 p	1-35 p	105 m.m.	Auchy.	Harley St.	10 Rounds.
11.	1-30 p	1-45 p	105 m.m.	,,	Vermelles.	
12.	1-45 p	2-55 p	105 m.m.	?	Spoil Bank.	
13.	1-30 p	3-40 p	105 m.m.	Haisnes.	Cambrin.	
14.	2-15 p	2-30 p	77 m.m.	?	Hollows.	
15.	3-25 p		150 m.m.	Auchy.	F 18 a 5.5	
16.	3-0 p		77 m.m.	?	A 2 front line.	
17.	3-30 p	3-45 p	77 m.m.	Auchy.	A 1	between Vauxhall & Westminster Bridges.
18.	,,		150 m.m.	Haisnes.	Canal.	
19.	4-35 p	5-0 p	77 m.m.	Auchy.	(A 21 d 1 3 (Russels Keep.	

* Unobserved fire - 5 blind.

Major, R.A.,

Brigade Major, R.A., 2nd Divn.

1509

DAILY AMMUNITION RETURN

DATE 24. XI. 15.

BATTERIES.

Piece	Projectile	Code	50	70	15	48	71	9	16	17	47	56	Total Per Piece
18-pr	Guns......												
	Shrapnel...	"A"	43	26	55	116	111	55	16	33			455
	H. E......	"Ax"	15	19	–	13	18	4	–	142			211
4.5"	Howitzers..												
	Shrapnel...	"B"									–	–	
	H. E......	"Bx"									14	106	120

2nd Division Artillery Orders

by

Brigadier-General G.H.SANDERS, D.S.O., Comdg.R.A., 2nd Divn.

24th November, 1915.

1135. COURTMARTIAL.

A F.G.C.M., composed as under, will assemble at 10-0a.m. on Saturday, 27th November, 1915 at Headquarters, R.A., 2nd Divn., 18 RUE SADI-CARNOT for the trial of 8829, Gr. R.Cairns, 16th Battery, R.F.A., 96812, Gr. A.Edmunds, 48th Battery, R.F.A., and 54234, Saddler G.Halstead, 48th Battery, R.F.A., and such other accused as may be brought before it :-

PRESIDENT.
Major E.W.Cushen. - 2nd Div. Amm. Column.

MEMBERS.
Captain D.C.Stephenson. - 17th Battery, R.F.A.
Lieutenant W.H.Brookes. - 56th Battery, R.F.A.

Accused to be warned and all witnesses duly requested to attend. 36th Brigade will find the Court Orderly.
Proceedings to be sent to Staff Captain, R.A., 2nd Divn.

1136. BRICKS.

In future any units requiring to draw bricks must apply to C.R.E. C.R.E. will give instructions from which stack bricks should be drawn and an order to draw.

1137. REPORTS - AMATOL.

Reference R.A.No.643 circulated on 12th instant.
Reports called for by 30th November, 1915, on results as regards detonation of Amatol, should be forwarded to this office by evening of 25th November, 1915.

L.G.BUXTON, Capt, R.A.

Staff Captain, R.A., 2nd Divn.

1511

GROUP DIARY.

B.

DATE - Nov 25TH 1915

Observation possible 8 AM. to 3.30 PM

General. The Heavy Howitzers firing in the neighbourhood of F18 a 5 4 yesterday appear from Bearings taken from the scoops and differences in Range to have fired from VIOLAINES True Bearing 70° from F18 a 5.4. At least two of these guns were firing.

To-day has been very quiet on this front.

Enemy's Works.
Enemy were observed working on their front trenches A 16 c 0 5 6 1 7

Action.

No.	Time. From.	To.	Battery.	Target.	Rounds.	Remarks.
(1)	4.20 PM	—	56	Enemy in open near CANTELEUX	8	Yesterday
(2)	9.12 PM	9.30 PM	"	MINNIE ACTIVE	12	"
(3)	11.17 AM	—	"	" "	14	Request of H.L.I.
(4)	2.45 PM	—	"	" "	8	
(5)	9.55 PM	10.10 PM	70	GUN FLASHES behind HAISNES CEMETERY	24	
~~(6)~~	~~10.10 PM~~				14	Retaliation
(6)	10.10 PM		70	Trenches just N of MAIN ROAD	9	Working Party
(7)	9 AM	—	70	A 21 c 6 7	20	To worry Transport
(8)	6 PM	8 PM	71	Roads round CANTELEUX	9	
(9)	9 PM	—	71	LA BASSÉE	12	Series fired by attached officers
(10)	1.10 PM		71	A 16 a 3.3	20	
(11)	3.15 PM		71	A 16 a 5.1		

B. Quiller Couch Lieut & Adj
for
Lieut. Colonel.
Commanding A Group.

B.

Z GROUP DIARY.

DATE - 25-11-15

General.

An attack was made by Germans on the crater they blew up and on GIBSONS crater at 9.15 pm. It was repulsed. 9th Batt fired on night lines about 50 rds. 17th Batt about 350 rds. There was firing at intervals all last night by 17th Batt.

Enemy's Works.

Smoke was observed in LES BRIQUES 17th Batt fired.

No fresh work observed.

17th Batt fired special series to instruct attached officers. Also another series to test AMATOL shell.

Action.

No.	Time. From.	To.	Battery.	Target.	Rounds.	Remarks.
1	Irregular intervals during night		9th	German 2nd line trenches.	about 250 rds	By request of infantry
2	2.45 pm		9th	" "	about 20 rds.	
3	4.15 pm on till	5.15 pm 12.15 am	17th 17	German trenches "	300 rds 100 rds	" "
4	10.35 am			"		"
5	11.20 am			Front line		
6	11.45 am			AUCHY		Instructional
7	12.30 pm			AUCHY		to test AMATOL
8	12.35			German front line		By request of inf.
9	2.30 pm and 3.45 pm			" "		" "
10	4.5 pm			LES BRIQUES		Smoke seen

Lieut. Colonel.
Commanding Group.

B.

GROUP DIARY,

DATE - 25-11-15

General.

Enemy's Works.

Action.

No.	Time From.	To.	Battery.	Target.	Rounds.	Remarks.
●	5.30pm		15th Batt.	MADAGASCAR Tr.	6	By request
12	8.15 am			" "	8	"
13	11.30 am					
14	11.45 am			LONE FARM	17	checking reg.
15	12.45 pm			MADAGASCAR Tr.	4	checking reg.
				" "	13	retaliation
16	3.45 pm			" "	4	"
17	3.30 pm			RAILWAY cottage	3	"
18	12 pm — 1pm		48th Batt	LONE FARM MINE Pt.	} Registration and destruction
19	2pm	3pm		LEANTO cottage Railway trench Popes nose	} By request
20	6.33 pm 10.10 pm 11.19 pm		47th Batt	{ FRANKS heap + A222 06 FRANKs heap	4 rds 15 rd	to stop MINE by order of Z
	12.16 am 1.15 am 2.30 am					

J. Rodd
Lieut. Colonel
Commanding Z Group.

2nd Division Hostile Fire Report.

25th November, 1915.

1. General Information.

50th Battery report enemy's 5.9" How. Battery which shelled F 18 a 5 4 and neighbourhood yesterday fired from VIOLAINES. True bearings from shell scrapings 70 deg. 71st Battery add that there were at least two guns of this battery firing. Very quiet day. Enemy far less active than yesterday.

Field gun located yesterday bearing 110 deg. Mag. from BRADDELL Castle fired yesterday afternoon and again last night at about 9-45 p.m. It is supposed that it is position marked in A 22 d central.

2 HOSTILE FIRE.

N	Time From To	Nature	Direction from.	Area shelled	Remarks,
1	10-10p-10-15,	77 mm	AUCHY	A 1	
2	9-55 a-10-10a	,,	HAISNES Cy	Z2 Support trens.	
3	10-30a	,,	AUCHY	A 21 d 1 9	2 rounds
4	10-45a	,,	,,	A 27 c 1 0	4 ,,
5	12-30p - 1-30p	,,	,,	Support trs near A 27 d	30 ,,
6	12-45p - 1 p	,,	,,	Trenches Z2	10 ,,
7	3-40p	,,	,,	Same as 5	3 ,,
8	3-55p	150 mm	?	PONT FIXE	1 ,,

G H Sanders Brig-General
C. R. A. 2nd Division.

Dispatched 6-35 pm

1513

DAILY AMMUNITION RETURN

DATE 25 Novr 1915

BATTERIES.

Piece	Projectile	Code	50	70	15	48	71	9	16	17	47	56	Total	Per Piece
18-pr	Guns......													
	Shrapnel...	"A"	44	24	117	137	95	206	17	525	–	–	1165	
	H. E......	"Ax"	77	23	–	13	25	64	–	300	–	–	502	
4.5"	Howitzers..													
	Shrapnel...	"B"												
	H. E......	"Bx"									31	73	104	

2nd Division Artillery Orders

by

Brigadier-General G.H.SANDERS, D.S.O., Comdg.R.A., 2nd Divn.

25th November, 1915.

1138. FUZE KEYS.

Indents for fuze keys Service Pattern to replace Gun Metal fuze keys Nos. 17, 18, and 42 should now be submitted where necessary.

A.DURAND, Lieut,R.A.,

a/Staff Captain, R.A., 2nd Divn.

1515

Z GROUP DIARY,

DATE - 26-11-15

B.

General.

Very little hostile shelling today. Light mainly unfavourable

Enemy's Works.

No fresh work observed.
Fire was observed behind Haines 11.25 am
a wooden cross has been erected about A.29.d.1½.9

Action.

No.	Time. From.	To.	Battery.	Target.	Rounds.	Remarks.
	5 pm	6 am	9th	Trenches behind new craters	about 9 rds	by request of infantry.
	5.15 pm		15th	Madagascar	4	at request of inf.
3	9.17 pm		—	—	9	—
4	12.5 pm		—	—	8	To prepare which was postponed
5	3 pm		—	LONE farm for wirecutting	11	owing to cloudy reg.
6	7 pm 11.25 pm 1.10 am 3.25 am 5.25 am 6.45 am 6.55 am		17th	night lines	150 rds	by request increased rate asked

over -

Lieut. Colonel.
Commanding Group.

7	11.30am		17th	Straw mound	20
				A22a9.2	
8	3.35pm		—	Trenches	16

9	8.54am	—	47th	A22c06 & A21B.7	4	By requests
	9am	—			8	of run
	11.38am	—			8	
	11.44am	—			12	
	11.55am	12.25am			12	
10	2.2pm	2.17pm		Junct MAD ALLEY & Petrie alley	7	registration

11	8pm	8.15pm	48th	AUCHY	40 shrap
12	8.15am	8.45am		Mine point	15 retaliation
13	11.30am	—		Trenches	4 rds to every
					Phizz bang. retaliation

71st Batt Registered Railway cottage
Madagascar
A29c 2.3.

F. Rodd Ln
Adj: Z group.

B.

GROUP DIARY,

DATE - NOV 26 1915

General. Observation possible 7.30 AM to 4.15 PM
ENEMY were very quiet except 10 AM
to 10.30 when most of the activity was to
north and south.
Heavy snow and hail 11.15 AM - 1.30 PM.
Light very good 1.30 PM to 3.30 PM.
ENEMY had BALLOON up in direction
of SALOME 2.30 PM to 4 PM.

Enemy's Works.

NIL

Action.

No.	Time. From.	Time. To.	Battery.	Target.	Rounds.	Remarks.
(1)	odd intervals through night		50	support trenches	39	Request of Infantry.
(2)	9.40 AM		56	ENEMY in open N of CANAL	?	
(3)	2.55 PM		56	A 16 a 8.6 NE Brickstack.	?	Working Party
(4)	3.45 PM		56	A 16 a 2.9		"
(5)	6 PM	10 PM	70	LA BASSEE ROAD near AUCHY		Working Party
(6)	2 PM		70	A 21 c 7.7		"
(7)	3.45 PM		70	"		Retaliation
(8)	9.45 AM		71	CANTELEUX & P⁺82	30	"
(9)	12.30 PM		71	DISTILLERY A 17 d	16	Request of Infantry.
(10)	2 PM		71	SNIPER'S POST	22	
(11)	9.30 AM	11 AM	MTN BTY	A 21 c 8.8 A 21 c 9.6 A 15 d 8.2 A 15 d 9.1	60	

B Quiller Couch
Lieut Adj
for Lieut. Colonel.
Commanding A Group.

2nd Divisional Artillery

HOSTILE FIRE REPORT.

26th November 1915.

1 General Information.

The enemy have been very quiet all day between LA BASSEE Road and GIVENCHY. Light was good for observation during the afternoon. Heavy hail and snow storms in the morning.

2 HOSTILE FIRE.

No.	Time From	To	Nature	Direction from	Aera shelled	Remarks.
1	8-15a	8-45a	77mm) 4.2" Howr.)	AUCHY	A 21 c 7 & Russells Keep	3 rds 77 mm 12 rds 4.2 How
2	8-55a	9-5a	5.9" How.	AUCHY	Front line	Opposite Rly. trench 3 rds.
3	10-35a	10-50a	77mm	AUCHY	Hollow & A2 Sec. trenches.	
4	11-25a	11-55a	4.2" Howr.	?	A 27 b 0 5	
5	3-30p		"Woolies" 4.2 Air	HAISNES	Commn trs Z1	4 rounds.

Major R.A.

Brigade Major R.A. 2nd Divn.

"A" Form.
Army Form C. 2121.
MESSAGES AND SIGNALS. No. of Message 1518

TO — 2nd Div G

Sender's Number: Bm 976 Day of Month: 16 AAA

Wire cutting this week aaa
2 groups at A28c 4 8
aaa A group just N
of LA BASSEE road aaa
at earliest ~~opportunity~~ favorable
opportunity 2 good nights
aaa

From: R.A. I Div
Place:
Time: 9 45 am

1577

DAILY AMMUNITION RETURN

DATE 26.XI.15

BATTERIES.

Piece	Projectile	Code	50	70	15	48	71	9	16	17	47	56	Total Per Piece
18-pr	Guns.......												
	Shrapnel...	"A"	48	10	44	102	57	52	17	162	—	—	492
	H. E.......	"Ax"	4	—	—	26	33	41	—	70	—	—	174
4.5"	Howitzers..												
	Shrapnel...	"B"									—	—	—
	H. E.......	"Bx"									40	11	51

2nd Division Artillery Orders

by

Brigadier-General G.H.SANDERS, D.S.O., Comdg.R.A., 2nd Divn.

26th November, 1915.

1139. REST HOUSE.

Attention is again drawn to 2nd Divn. R.O., No.2. dated 22nd November, 1915, with reference to the position of the new Rest House for men proceeding on leave.

1140. PROMOTIONS.

No. 33423, Sergt P.Daley, 41st B.A.C., and No. 12419, Sergt.A.E.Smart, 71st Battery, to be B.S.M's in 2nd Division Ammunition Column, with effect from 18th November,1915, to complete establishments. To join D.A.C. forthwith. *No. 27068, Sergt.W.B.Clarke to B.Q.M.S.in 15th Divn.Arty.26-11-15, (to proceed (forthwith.

1141. COURTMARTIAL.

No. 59011, Gr. J.Dixon and No. 29652, Dr. W.Winters, 15th Battery will be tried by the F.G.C.M. ordered to assemble by R.A.O., No.1135 of 24th instant.

1142. TRAFFIC.

Serious blocking of traffic has been occurring on the BEUVRY-BETHUNE and BETHUNE-CHOCQUES-LILLERS Roads. Traffic must rigidly adhere to the speed limits. Greater attention should be paid to march discipline. The time at which batteries intend using the above roads should always be reported to this Headquarters.

1143. CASUALTIES.

A Quarterly return showing the names of all men who have been dealt with for self-inflicted wounds should reach this office on the 2nd January, 2nd April, 2nd July and 2nd October. It should be stated how each case has been dealt with.

1144. APPOINTMENTS.

The following S.S.Corporals are appointed Farrier Sergeants with effect from this date and posted to units as stated :-

No.34759. S.S.Corpl.H.Gibbard, 17th Battery to 70th Brigade,R.F.
No. 2973. S.S.Corpl.A.Weeks,34th B.A.C. to 71st Brigade, R.F.A.
No.60835. S.S.Corpl.L.G.Rook, 41st B.A.C. to 72nd Brigade,R.F.A.

These N.C.O's should be sent to join their new units at once. Authority R.A., 3rd Echelon, 13985, d/24-11-1915.

* Authority R.A., 3rd Echelon, 13984. d/24-11-1915.

A.DURAND, Lieut. R.A.,

a/Staff Captain, R.A., 2nd Divn.

T519

GROUP DIARY.

B.

DATE – Nov 27TH 1915

General. The Enemy have been reported by all Batteries as having fires in their 2ND line but practically no smoke coming from their first line. This points to the fact that they live generally in 2ND line and have their chief dugouts there. ENEMY have done some new work on Embankment redoubt.

Enemy's Works. Enemy had an Aeroplane up 12.40 PM to 12.55 PM quite near our line and it was not engaged (50TH BTY)

Observation possible 7.15 AM to 4 PM light good.

Wire cut last week A 21 C 15 is still unmended in places.

Action.

No.	Time From.	Time To.	Battery.	Target.	Rounds.	Remarks.
(1)	12	1 PM	MTN BTY	Enfilading trenches just N of LA BASSEE road	38	
(2)	2.30 PM	3.30 PM	"	Brickstacks and strong points in rear	42	4 direct hits on large dug out
(3)	10.30 AM		56	ENEMY in open near CANTELEUX		
(4)	10.40 AM		56	2ND line A 21 d.		
(5)	11.20 AM		50	Working Party A 21 C.5		Repairing Front line.
(6)	3.30 PM		50	EMBANKMENT REDOUBT		
(7)	6 PM	10 PM	70	LA BASSEE Road		Intermittent working party
(8)	2.5 PM	2.50 PM	70	{A 21 b 7.7 {A 21 b 8.8		"
(9)	3 PM			A 21 a 5.9		
(10)	6 PM	8 PM	71	Roads around CANTELEUX	20	Intermittent Working Party
(11)	10.45 AM		71	A 16 a 2.3	15	
(12)	1 PM	2 PM	71	SNIPER'S POST CANAL TRENCH	40	A request of Infantry who observed & satisfied

B. Quiller Couch
Lieut & Adj

for Lieut. Colonel.
Commanding A Group.

B.

Z GROUP DIARY,

DATE - 27-11-15

General.

Signalling with lamps in DOUVRIN again seen. No message was sent from the station; they were apparently receiving one. 1.15 pm

Enemy's Works.

Fresh wire seems to have been placed in front of Fosse Trench from A28d07 to junction of Fosse tr. and CORON alley.

Action.

No.	Time. From.	To.	Battery.	Target.	Rounds.	Remarks.
1	8.30am		9th Batt	LONE FARM	10	Working party dispersed.
2	9am	12 noon		Various points in front line	30 rds	Instruction
3	1 pm	1.30pm		Bursts of fire front trenches	30	retaliation
4	2 pm			Suspected O.P. A23a0.5		with HE.
5	2.30pm			Trenches	10 rds	retaliation
6	4.15pm			Trenches N of road	10 rds	at request of infantry who were out of comm. with 56th + 70th
7	9.40am		15th Batt	Madagascar tr	4	Retaliation
8	11.30am			Mad alley	9	checking reg.
9	12.00 noon			Support tr A21b	7	registration
10	12.30pm			Madagascar tr.	4	retaliation
11	1 pm			QUARRY tr	13	Registration
12	1.15pm			" "	5	"
13	2.40pm	3 pm		New trench	20	Checking "

over

Lieut. Colonel.
Commanding Group.

14	8.40 am 9.55 am	17th Batt	Working parties 25 rds	
15	11. am		Front tr. 9 retaliation	
16	2.25 pm		SNIPERS Post 15 movement & periscope seen	
17	2.55 pm		Front trenches 18 retaliation	
18	1.6 pm 1.12 pm	47th How. Batt.	A22 C 06 A21 d 8.7	3 checking reg.
19	2.15 pm 2.45 pm	—	— LES BRIQUES 10	suspected gun position.
20	11.30 am	48th Batt	MINE pt 18	retaliation to Minnie.
21	11.45 am		RAILWAY A28a	20 registration
22	2.30 pm 3.30 pm		{ Lone pine and Forse Support tr. Forse cottages Mine point	retaliation and offence.

F. Rodd
Adj't Z group

2nd Divisional Artillery

HOSTILE FIRE REPORT.

27th November, 1915.

Hostile Fire.

No.	Time. From	To	Nature.	Direction from	Area shelled.	Remarks.
1.	9-15 a		77 m.m.	Auchy.	Trenches A 27b 4 2	2 Rounds.
2.	9-30 a	10-0 a	4.2" How.	Violaines.	Givenchy X roads.	
3.	11-0 a	11-15 a	77 m.m.	?	,,	
4.	11-0 a	11-30 a	4.2" How.	?	Z2 front tr.	a few.
			77 m.m.	?	Z2 front tr.	20 Rounds.
5.	12-20 p		77 m.m.	Auchy.	Cuinchy.	
6.	12-30 p		77 m.m.	Auchy.	A 27b 4 2	2 Rounds.
7.	12-50 p	1-5 p	4.2" How.	Auchy.	A1 Trenches.	
8.	1-50 p		77 m.m.	Auchy.	Hollow.	Probably in retaliation.
9.	2-55 p	3-30 p	4.2" How.	?	Z2 trench	18 Rounds.
10.	3-0 p		77 m.m.	La Bassee.	Canal.	
11.	3-0 p		4.2" How.	Violaines.	Pont Fixe.	

No.4 probably in retaliation to our 8" Howitzers.

Major, R.A.,
Brigade Major, R.A., 2nd Divn.

SECRET.

R.A.
T/27

H.Q., 2nd Division.

In reply to 2nd Division G.S.746:
1. <u>Auxiliary means of communication in use betw</u>
<u>and batteries supporting them-nil.</u>

2. <u>Means which have been tried</u> -
   (a) Between firing line and observing stations.
      (i) Coloured discs kept by infantry at pre-ar
visible from observation posts. The discs are of
according to a pre-arranged simple code signifying
company or battalion, lift fire and retaliate. Th
into use in case of a breakdown in telephone wires
      (ii) Lamps. The lamp, which is sufficiently
used by day, shows a ray in any but the clearest
this reason the same lamps will not do. By nigh
electric lamps cannot be improved on.
   (b) Between observing stations and batteries.
Flags by day - Lamps by day and night. A syste
sort is wherever possible maintained during oper
as it is found that with triplicate lines, inte
frequent checking of all lines and immediate rep
telephone system does not break down, these alte
systems are not regularly maintained.
      Their use necessitates the constant atten
observers in addition to telephone men.

3. <u>Suggestions for improvement of communi</u>
   (a) A system of Group Exchanges has been
Division. One is almost complete in Z Grou
exchange has been arranged at the battle
well protected against all classes of shel
each battery and observing station in the
Group H.Q. It is hoped to make connect
ing Group Exchanges. The infantry batta
left connected direct with their corres
stations, but they too may be brought i
objects are facility in switching fire
being run out for observers, saving of
wire.
   (b) For better maintenance of wires
special trenches. This would result
quiet times, but also in easy repair
are fully employed with traffic.
   (c) For alternative communication b
and observing stations, it is suggest
provide for the simplest needs. Ther
messages infantry want to send -
         Call for support (atta
         Lift fire.
         Retaliate fo
To meet this a lamp
could be put up at batta
seen from the observing
This system would be ea
system and could be mad
by day.
   (d) The Observing Sta
invariably be treated
requirements. The ol
rarely be possible t
unless the country

Inst/36a.
27-11-1915.

Z Group.
A Group.
H.A., 1st Corps.
2nd Divn, G.S.   } For information.

B.M. Inst. 36a.   27th November, 1915.

Inst.36 is cancelled.

2. In order to carry into effect the Corps Commander's wish to locate, and to damage, hostile guns with concentrated fire the following will be the procedure.

3. In the case where a Group Commander considers the opportunity to be a passing one: he will open fire with his own group getting such co-operation from heavies and neighbouring groups as the opportunity admits.

4. In the case where the opportunity is not a passing one, and the hostile battery is judged unlikely to move: it should be observed until accurately located, by cross bearings if possible, even if several days pass during this observation. R.A., H.C., will be informed, and the co-operation of neighbouring groups and of H.A., 1st Corps secured. During this time the target should not be fired on, inorder that it may not be discouraged from betraying itself. When good observation is got other observers should be informed of the observing station from which it can be seen. In this way all concerned will be fully informed and ready to open fire at half an hour's notice when it again is active and the personnel exposed.

5. Extract from Corps instructions repeated :-
"The Corps Commander wishes special efforts made to locate hostile guns estimated within 9000 yards of our trenches. After such a gun or guns have been accurately located, directly they re-open fire the Divisional Artillery Commander in whose area the target is situated will arrange to engage it on the following plan - Every gun and howitzer under his command whose arc of fire permits will fire for two minutes with H.E.".

Major, R.A.,
Brigade Major, R.A., 2nd Divn.

SECRET.   2nd Division No. G.S.759/1.

1st Army.
_____

No.597 (G). 27th November, 1915.
_____

A minor artillery operation will be carried out on 28th November and 29th November with a view to destroying mine shafts in the vicinity of A.21.d.

The following artillery will be employed :-

2 - 9.2" Howitzers.   )   When not taking calls from the
2 - 8"   ,,   )   air for counter-battery work.

The 50th Battery consisting of 2 - 6" Howitzers.

The artillery of the 2nd Division as required.

(sd) A.S.Cobbe, Brigadier-General,
for Lieut-General,
Commanding 1st Corps.

(2)

2nd Division.
_____

With reference to above, the 2 sections of heavy howitzers are placed at your disposal for the above operations.

(sd) A.S.Cobbe, Bdr-General,
27-11-15.   General Staff, 1st Corps.

(3)

R.A., 2nd Division.
_____

For information and necessary action, please.

These Howitzers will be under your command.

2nd Division.   Major,
27th November, 1915.   General Staff, 2nd Divn.

"A" Form. Army Form C. 2121.
MESSAGES AND SIGNALS.

Prefix	Code	m.	Words	Charge	This message is on a/c of	Recd. at	m.
Office of Origin and Service Instructions.			Sent			Date	
Secret			At	m.	Service	From	
SR			To				
			By		(Signature of "Franking Officer.")	By	

TO: ~~5th Bde~~ ~~RE~~ ~~15th Div~~
    ~~6th Bde~~ ~~1st Corps~~
    ~~RA~~   ~~7th Div~~

| Sender's Number. | Day of Month | In reply to Number | |
| GA 81 | 27 | | AAA |

1st Corps has placed Corps artillery at disposal of 2nd Div on 28th and 29th Nov for bombardment of German trenches opposite ETNA aaa Details of bombardment have been communicated to all concerned aaa 5th and 6th Inf Bdes will at 9 am each day commence clearing front line between Boyau 17 and TOWER TRENCH both inclusive unless warned by R.A.Z group commander that day is not favourable for bombardment aaa Infantry between above limits will be withdrawn to line HIGH STREET - ST PATRICK TRENCH - BACK STREET - SHORT CUT aaa Bombardment will commence as soon as infantry notify to R A Z group commander that front line is clear probably about 10 am aaa In view of expected retaliation all reliefs on 28th and 29th will be carried

From
Place
Time

"A" Form.
MESSAGES AND SIGNALS.

Army Form C. 2121.

Prefix	Code	m.	Words	Charge	This message is on a/c of	No. of Message
Office of Origin and Service Instructions.						Recd. at .... m.
			Sent		.... Service.	Date ....
			At .... m.			From ....
			To			
			By		(Signature of "Franking Officer.")	By ....

TO

Sender's Number.	Day of Month	In reply to Number	AAA

out before 10 am or after 3 pm aaa Work on 2nd and 3rd lines under RE supervision will be suspended on 28th and 29th aaa RA Z group commander is responsible for informing infantry each day at once when bombardment is finished and front line may again be re-occupied aaa addressed 5th 6th Bdes RA RE repeated 1st corps 7th Div and 15th Div for information

From **2nd Div**
Place
Time **11. am**

Louis Vaughan Lt Col

The above may be forwarded as now corrected. (Z)

Censor. Signature of Addressor or person authorised to telegraph in his name.

* This line should be erased if not required.

SECRET

COPY No. 12.

2nd Divisional Artillery Operation Order No.9.

Reference Trench Map - 1/10,000 36cN.W.1.
and
1/5,000 36c N.W.1. W.half.

27th November, 1915.

1. The Divisional Artillery will carry out a bombardment, according to the attached table, of a portion of the enemy's line opposite Z2 section on 28th and 29th instant if weather conditions are favourable.

2. A portion of the H.A., 1st Corps has been placed at the disposal of 2nd Division and will co-operate according to instructions which have been issued separately.

3. 47th and 56th Howitzer Batteries and 59th Siege Battery are placed under the orders of O.C., Z Group for these operations.

4. O.C., Z Group will, after consultation with O.C., 10th Siege Battery, arrange with G.O.C.,5th and 6th Infantry Bdes for all infantry to be withdrawn from that portion of the line, between BOYAU 17(inc.) and TOWER TRENCH(inc.) to the line HIGH STREET-ST.PATRICK'S Trench-BACK STREET-SHORT CUT.
    The bombardment will open as soon as the infantry are clear.
    He will also inform G.O.C., 6th Brigade when the heavy bombardment is closed.

5. Should the heavy bombardment be discontinued owing to bad weather the night firing will be opened and continued as the 6th Infantry Brigade Commander may desire.

Major, R.A.,

Brigade Major, R.A., 2nd Division.

Issued at   to :-
    Copy No.1. Z Group.
    ,,   2. A Group.
    ,,   3. 44th Brigade.
    ,,   4. 34th   "
    ,,   5. 59th Siege Battery.
    ,,   6. D.A.C.
    ,, 7&8. 2nd Division.G.S.)
    ,,   9. H.A., 1st Corps.   )
    ,,   10. R.A., 7th Division.) For information.
    ,,   11. R.A.,15th Division.)

No.	Battery.	Time.	Target.	Ammunition.	Remarks.
1.	2 18-pdr Batteries (Z Group)	9-0 a.m. to 10-0 a.m.	On line A 27 b 9 9 - A 21 b 9 3.	10 rounds per battery per hour.	
2.	1 18-pdr. Battery & 2 Sections (Z Group)	10-0 a.m. to 4-0 p.m.	A 27 b 6 10-8 7. A 21 d 8 3 - A 27 b 10 8. A 21 d 10 10 - 10 3. A 21b 5 0-7 4.	90 rounds per hour.	Intermittent.
3.	59th Siege	10-0 a.m. to 3-0 p.m.	A 21d 7 8-7 9.	200 rounds.	
4.	47th How. Battery 56th How. Battery	10-0 a.m. to 4-0 p.m.	FRANKs KEEP RYANS KEEP A 21d 8 4-7 9.	)) 40 rounds) per hour.	Intermittent.
5.	2 18-pdr. Batteries. (Z Group).	4-0 p.m. to 10-0 a.m.	As in 1.	10 rounds per battery per hour.	Intermittent.

On the second day the programme will be repeated.

DAILY AMMUNITION RETURN

DATE 27. XI. 15

BATTERIES.

Piece	Projectile	Code	50	70	15	48	71	9	16	17	47	56	Total Per Piece
18-pr	Guns.......												
	Shrapnel...	"A"	20	8	40	162	120	50	14	40	-	-	454
	H. E.......	"Ax"	-	8	-	4	13	22	2	47	-	-	96
4.5"	Howitzers..												
	Shrapnel...	"B"									-	-	-
	H. E.......	"Bx"									11	56	67

2nd Divisional Artillery Orders

by

Brigadier-General G.H.SANDERS, D.S.O., Comdg.R.A.,2nd Divn.

27th November,1915.

1145. DIVINE SERVICE.

Services will be held to-morrow,28th November,1915, as under :-

(a), CHURCH OF ENGLAND.

IN THE UNFINISHED CHAPEL, RUE D'AIRE.

10-0 a.m.   For all R.F.A.Units in or near BETHUNE.

Voluntary Service :-

6-0 p.m.   Evening Service, (followed by Sacred Concert).

(b), ROMAN CATHOLIC.

BETHUNE CATHEDRAL.   10-30 a.m.

(c). WESLEYANS and FREE CHURCH. at 6-0 p.m.

Divisional Recreation Room, RUE D'AIRE.

A.DURAND, Lieut,R.A.,
a/Staff Captain, R.A.2/Divn.

B.

GROUP DIARY,

DATE – Nov 28TH 1915

General. Observation possible 7.15 AM till 4 PM

Enemy's Artillery were quiet all day and only replied with Field guns to our Bombardment.

Enemy's Works. Enemy were observed working in his trenches A 16 c 1.7

Action.

No.	Time From.	To.	Battery.	Target.	Rounds.	Remarks.
(1)	9.30 AM		50	Enemy trenches	7	Retaliation
(2)	11.30 AM		50	" "	6	working party
(3)	3 PM		50	A 16 c 1.7	6	under 2 group
(4)	10 AM	4 PM	56	Trenches A 21 d	114	
(5)	3.30 PM		56	ENEMY in open A 10 d 7.7	3	
(6)	9.25 AM		70	A 21 b 8.7	18	Retaliation
(7)	3.30 PM		70	"	4	"
(8)	9.15 AM		71	CANTELEUX	10	
(9)	9.45 AM	10.15 AM	71	A 16 a 5.3 to 7.8	15	Registration for flank support
(10)	3.30 PM		71	LORGIES RD	8	

B. Quiller Couch
Lieut & Adj
for Lieut. Colonel.
Commanding A Group.

B.

Z GROUP DIARY,

DATE - 28-11-15

General.

There was much less retaliation than was anticipated. see report.

German aeroplanes up this morning, retarded progress considerably our machines did not seem to frighten them. - Our trenches were only damaged in one place, in HOLLOWAY. GIBSON's crater was not damaged but the german crater opposite has been considerably disturbed and is visible from GIBSONS cra.sap. This sap is also undamaged. Trenches were examined at 3.20pm. There was no rifle sniping, loophole plates were all closed and no periscopes were visible. On looking over Backpt parapet O.C. 9th Batt was "sniped" by field gun 2 rds salvos Their O.P. is thought to be in trenches A 21 b 7.1
over

Action.

No.	Time. From.	Time. To.	Battery.	Target.	Rounds.	Remarks.
1	10 am	3.59 pm	9th	Programm	6 rds per hour	
2	11 am		9th	A 23 a 5.8	suspected guns.	Shelling Bradell pt. ceased.
3	10 am	3 pm	15th	Programm	intermittent bursts.	
4	3.50 pm	still firing	17th	Program as ordered relieving 9th Battery		
5	10 am	3 pm	48th	Program as ordered	8 rds per hour and bursts.	
6	7.45 pm 27/11/15			HAINES	18 rds	
7	11 pm	"		"	8 rds	
8	2 pm 28/11/15			MADAGASCAR	10 rds	5 HE & Shrap
9	2.45 h			Railway cottage	"	"
10	3.30 p			Transvaal	"	"

Lieut.Colonel.
Commanding Group.

During the bombardment however pieces of metal from our shell were being thrown some distance, one piece landed near Ridge H0.

11	10 am	4 pm	47th	FRANKS heap, Ryans heap, A'21 d support tr	121 rds program
12	10 am	4 pm	71st Det Sect.	Railway tr Support trench	bursts of fire
12	12 noon 27/11/15 12 noon 28/11/15			Railway tr	85 rds

Rodd
Adj. 41st Bde

2nd Divisional Artillery

HOSTILE FIRE REPORT.

28th November 1915.

No.	Time From — To	Nature	Direction from	Aera shelled	REMARKS.
	27th				
1	9-20p 9-28p	77mm	AUCHY	A 21 b 3 6 to 3.6	A few rounds
	28th				
2	9-10a 10-15a	10.5cm	—	PONT FIXE & WINDY Cr.	30 rounds
3	10-20a 10-30a	4.2" How	? a few	Z2 front tr.	) Mistaken for Brit.) shell by Infantry.
4	10-25a	5.9" How	? 2 rounds	RUSSELS Kp.	)
5	11a	77mm	AUCHY	BRADDELL Pt	20 rounds
6	11a 11-30a	77mm	AUCHY	,,	2 rds per minute.
7	11-30a	77mm	AUCHY	Trench A 21 b Z1	10 rounds
8	11-45a	4.2" How	?	,,	6 rounds
9	1 p.	77mm	?	HARPERS Kp	6 rounds
10	2-30p	77mm or 4.2"How	?	A 21c 5.5	10 rounds
11	3 p	77mm	?	A 21d 2.6	10 rounds
12	3-25p	10.5cm	?	A 21b 4.5	2 rounds

Major R.A.

Brigade Major R.A. 2nd Division

"A" Form.   Army Form C. 2121.
MESSAGES AND SIGNALS.   No. of Message_____

Prefix ___ Code ___ m.	Words	Charge	This message is on a/c of:	Recd. at ___ m.
Office of Origin and Service Instructions.	Sent			Date
	At ___ m.		Service.	From
	To			By
	By		(Signature of "Franking Officer.")	

TO { H₁ 1ˢᵗ Corps

Sender's Number	Day of Month	In reply to Number	A A A
Bm 928	28		

4 Bde report gun which
fired at BRADDELL PT is
probably near PLUM TREE HO
aaa 9ᵗʰ Battery turned on
to that neighbourhood whereupon
it ceased aaa 71ˢᵗ Battery
locate a howitzer battery firing
on towards VERMELLES at
A 18 b 1.5 aaa

From RA 2 Div
Place
Time 7.30 pm

The above may be forwarded as now corrected.   (Z)
Censor.   Signature of Addressor or person authorised to telegraph in his name.
This line should be erased if not required.

R.A., 2nd Division Situation - 28-11-1915.

GROUP.	UNIT.	BATTERY POSITION.	WAGON LINE.
-	34th Brigade H.Q.		BETHUNE (Rue St.Pry).
A.	50th Battery.	F 18a 3 2.	F 13c 9 9.
A.	70th Battery.	F 24c 9 2.	F 13c 9 9.
A.	36th Brigade H.Q.	A 19d 3 2.	
Z.	15th Battery.	L 8a 0 5.	F 14a 5 2.
Z.	48th Battery.	A 19d 1 1.	F 14a 5 2.
A.	71st Battery.	F 18a 8 8.(4)	E 5a 5 10.
Z.		A 24c 2 6.(2)	
Z.	41st Brigade H.Q.	A 19d 5 3.	
Z.	9th Battery.	F 18c 3 1.	F 7a 7 8.
H.A.	16th Battery.	F 24a 3 6.	W 26b 3 3.
Z.	17th Battery.	F 24a 3 2.	F 13d 2 10.
-	44th Brigade H.Q.		BETHUNE.
Z.	47th Battery.	F 30c 6 2.	W 21c 9 2.
A.	56th Battery.	A 20a 5 2.	CHAMP DE MARS.
Z. A.	7th Mountain Bty.	{ A 20a 6 4.(2) (A 26d 9 2.(2)	F 8b.
-	59th Siege Battery.	F 30c 5 6.	- -
-	34th B.A.C.		E 18b 5 5.
-	36th B.A.C.		W 29b 5 8.
-	41st B.A.C.		E 18b 9 3.
-	44th B.A.C.		CHAMP DE MARS.
-	D.A.C.		E 21a.

DAILY AMMUNITION RETURN

DATE 28. XI. 15.

BATTERIES.

Piece	Projectile	Code	50	70	15	48	71	9	16	17	47	56	Total Per Piece
18-pr	Guns.......												
	Shrapnel...	"A"	39	44	47	88	47	92	32	14			403
	H. E.......	"Ax"	-	27	37	103	58	250	7	77			559
4.5"	Howitzers..												
	Shrapnel...	"B"									1	-	1
	H. E.......	"Bx"									46	36	82

B.

Z GROUP DIARY,

DATE - 29-11-15

General.
There was rather more hostile retaliation today than yesterday. As yesterday german shells falling were reported as ours falling short. One heavy shell did fall short at 2.50 pm however in Bazan and damaging the trench. 1st Kings (Liverpool) regt. sent out patrol after the bombardment to investigate.

Enemy's Works.
Many of the german 4.2" were blind today and some did not detonate well.

WORK Enemy has thrown out more fresh earth along tr from railway to A28 b 45; 35.
Much fresh concertina wire has been placed South of MAD point.

Action.

No.	Time. From:	To:	Battery.	Target.	Rounds.	Remarks.
1	10 am	3 pm	9th	Program	60 rds per hour	
2	3.30 pm	3.50 pm		"	40 rds per hour	
3	10 am	3 pm	15th	Program as ordered.		
4	10.5 am	10.15 am		Madagascar tr + support	7	retaliation
5	10.30 am			Suspected OP A23c5.8	9	"
6	11.30 am			new tr A28 Central	26	"
7	12.30 pm	1 pm		Madagascar tr + support	21	"
8	2.30 pm	3.30 pm		" "	140	"
9	3.50 pm 28/11/15	10 am 29/11/15	17	Program as ordered		
10	3.40 pm	—		" "	"	"

Lieut. Colonel.
Commanding Group.

11	10 am	4 pm	47th program as ordered 121 rds
12	10 am	4 pm	48th program as ordered.
13	12 noon		MINE point 10 retaliation
14	1.30pm 3.30pm		MINE point / 50r. retaliation POPES nose Railway tr Minenwerfer A21d63
15	10 am	4 pm	71st Section program as ordered.
16	3 pm		MINE point 6 retaliation

F. Rodd
Adj. 41½ Dn.

GROUP DIARY.

B.

DATE - Nov 29th 1915

General. Observation possible 7 AM to 3.45 PM.
There was a certain amount of bombing and counter bombing near EMBANKMENT REDOUBT.
Enemy's Artillery were not active north of LA BASSÉE ROAD.

Enemy's Works.

"NIL"

Action.

No.	Time. From.	Time. To.	Battery.	Target.	Rounds.	Remarks.
(1)	10 P		50	EMBANKMENT REDOUBT	3	Request of Infantry
(2)	9.15 P	3.57 A	56	MINNENWERFER	34	
(3)	10 AM	4 PM	56	A 21 d	130	Bombardment
(4)	3.45 P		56	EMBANKMENT	7	Retaliation
(5)	6 PM	9.50 PM	70	LA BASSÉE RD	10	Transport
(6)	9.15 AM		70	C & D BRICKSTACKS	3	Retaliation
(7)	7.30 PM		71	A 18 c 1.5 to A 12 c 7.3	12	
(8)	3.20 PM	3.30 PM	71	SNIPERS POST & M G EMPLACEMENT in Tortoise	16	Timber thrown up Material set on fire by HE.
(9)	10 AM	12 noon	MTN BTY	Enfilade Brickstacks	19	

B. B. Quiller Couch.
Lieut & Adj
for Lieut. Colonel.
Commanding A Group.

2nd Divisional Artillery.

HOSTILE FIRE REPORT.

29th November, 1915.

No.	Time From	To	Nature.	Direction from	Area shelled.	Remarks.
1.	9-15a		4.2"Time H.E.	LA BASSEE	3 Stack	2 rounds
2	10-25	12-30p	77mm	AUCHY ? & VIOLAINES	Trenches Z1 & Z2	Intermittently
3	10-40a	1-p	4.2"How	VIOLAINES	,,	Starting at Stafford Redt worked S to VERMELLES-AUCHY road.
4	12-30p	2-30p	77mm	VIOLAINES ?	,,	Reduced in rate
5	2-30p	3-30p	77mm or 4.2" How	? probably as above	Just S of LA BASSEE road.	renewed activity
6	2-30p	3-30p	4.2"How ?	?	A 27 c & d	Fairly heavy shelling
7	3-30p	4-p	77mm only	Same as 5	LA BASSEE rd	
8	3-40p	3-55p	4.2" How	-	S W of CUINCHY	Mostly blind 8 rounds.

2-50p One of our heavy shells fell short in BOYAU Z1 at least it is presumed to be ours.

A Durand Lt
officer for

Major R.A.

Brigade Major R.A. 2nd Divn.

2nd Divisional Artillery Orders

by

Brigadier-General G.H. SANDERS, D.S.O., Comdg, R.A., 2nd Divn.

29th November, 1915.

1146. R.A. ORDERS.

Were not issued yesterday, 28th November, 1915.

1147. TOBACCO - ISSUE OF

Units will report as early as possible to this office whether it is wished to replace the present issue of soft tobacco by hard, and if so, to what extent.

A. DURAND, Lieut. R.A.,

a/Staff Captain, R.A., 2nd Divn.

DIARY.

DATE 30th November 1915

OBSERVATION CONDITIONS. Light good. Observation possible 8 a.m.

WORK DONE BY ENEMY. A new work is in progress - trench A22d 1.4 to LEAN TO COTTAGE.
Large new work A5 c 5.6
Repairs to trenches and wire A16 a 2.9, A16 c 3.5
Repairs to wire in Z1.

MOVEMENT SEEN.
Working parties A23 c 2.3, A19 a 1.4, Front System Z2,
A22 a 5.5, A30 d 0.5, A21 d 5.0. LEAN TO COTTAGE.

GUNS LOCATED OR SUSPECTED.
A17 b 0.½ active.
A9 d 9½.3 — flash seen from A8 a 8.2   10 a.m.
A18 a 1.1 — flash seen from COWL H0.   12.30 p.m.

WORK DONE BY US.
One gun 7" Mountain Battery moved to position near Woburn Abbey.

GENERAL.
A certain amount of artillery activity by enemy. They bombarded Church Keep West, apparently in retaliation for our bombardment. Fragments took the form of rectangular pieces 3"×½" and do not seem of such good quality as our shell, which have rougher fragments. Detonations good. Bombardment ineffective, redoubt not being hit.
New pattern of shell noticed - diameter excl. driving band 4". Driving band ⅓ way up shell. Shell unpainted.
Two telescopes were seen at A21 b 5.8.
German infantry very quiet.

ACTION.   See Over.   Lt. Colonel.
                                    Commanding

ACTION Time From	To	Battery	Target	Rounds	Remarks
10a	11am	9	Working parties		dispersed
9p			A23 a 23 - working party		dispersed
2.10			A 19 1.4 - working party		dispersed
3.53p			" "		"
1.0a		15	Madagascar tr.	3	at infantry request
9.30a			Auchy	10	checking lines
8.30a			Madagascar tr.	15	retaliation
11a			"	9	"
11.40			"	5	"
12			"	4	"
12			Les Briques	15	registration
1.30p			Madagascar tr.	21	retaliation
10.55		17	Lone Farm w.p.	10	dispersed
11.5			Pekin tr. "	10	"
2.30p			Z2 w.p.		"
2.55			" "		"
9.25		47	A22 d 8.7 houses	8	dispersed
12.45	1.30p		A2 a 5.6 w.p.	13	"
3.37	3.42		A 30 d 0.5 w.p.	8	"
6.30p		48	Auchy	15	
7.45p			Douvrin	3	
7.10a			A 21 d 5.0 w.p.		Fire put out
7.45a			Ryans Keep		retaliation
7.50			Mine Point	20	registration
9.30	11		Château alley	20	"
11.75	12		Hindenburg tr.	15	retaliation
2.30p			Mine Point	5	Work Stopped
3.15p			Lean to Cottage w.p.		
6.30p		71	Auchy	8	
7.50a			Railway tr.	4	retaliation
10a			Madagascar tr.	10	"
3.30p			"	5	
7.50		50	Embankment Redt.	20	retaliation
8.34		56	"	11	"
9.55		56	False Culvert	5	movement
10.40	11.30	56	New Work A 5 c 5 6	29	retaliation
1p		56	Embankment dent	12	"
9.20a		70	A 16 d 7.5	14	"
1p		70	A 21 b 8.8	20	Telescopes seen
7.35a	7.50	71	Canteleux	15	Retaliation
8	8.30	71	A 16 a 2.9	10	"
1.40	3.50	59 S	A 16 a 5½ 0 A 16 c 2 9 A 16 c 3	48	registration

2nd Divisional Artillery.
HOSTILE FIRE REPORT.

30th November, 1915.

Hostile Fire.

No.	Time From.	Time To.	Nature.	Direction from.	Area shelled.	Remarks.
1.	7-15a	8-15a	77mm	-	A 9 d 5.5	50 rounds
2	7-45a	8-45a	,,	AUCHY	COWL House	1 O.P. damaged no casualties.
3.	8-30a	8-40a	105mm	AUCHY	A 27 d	8 rounds
4.	8-45a	9-0a	77mm	,,	A 27 d 4.0 to 8.8	12 rounds
5.	8-45a	9-45a	77mm	-	A 9 c 0.5	50 rounds
6	9-30a	10-10a	,,	N of Canal	MAISON ROUGE ridge	20; 1 every 5min.
7.	10-0a	10-10a	105mm	?	CUINCHY	
8	10-0a		,,	A 18 d 9½.3	-	Flashes seen from A 8 d 8.2
9	11-0a	2-30p	5.9	?	A 25 b 6.9	
10	1-0a	1-30p	105 or 155mm	? DOUVRIN	A 19 d 5.2	* 45 rds per hour
11	11-3a	11-10a	77mm	?	A 27 a	5 rounds
12	11-45a	11-50a	105mm	?	Opposite MINE Point.	3 rounds
13	12-50p	1-20p	,,	?	COWL House	6; blind.
14	12-50p		77mm	A 18 a 1.1	-	Flashes seen from COWL House.
15	1-30p	2-0p	77mm	A U C H Y	A 28 c	20 rounds
16						

* Stopped when British Aeroplane went over.

A Durand Lt.
ofBERA for Major R.A.
Brigade Major R.A. 2nd Division.

R A

2ND DIV

The mountain Battery report has just come in and is also forwarded.

10.30 AM to noon fired 35 rounds Trenches and Tracks in front of Triangle

2.30 PM - 3.30 PM fired 56 rounds enfilading reserve trenches and into Triangle

30/11/15

B Quiller Couch
Lieut & Adjt
36 BDE RFA

Rec'd 9.30pm 30"/15

Headquarters,

2nd Division.

2nd Divisional Artillery and 1st Corps Heavy Artillery carried out a bombardment of the German trenches and mining works in Z2 Section on November 28th and 29th.

Guns employed -
- 9.2" Howitzers - 2.
- 8"   ,,   - 2.
- 6"   ,,   - 2.
- 4.5" ,,   - 2 batteries.
- 18-pdrs. guns. - 1 battery and 2 sections.

The Heavy Howitzers bombarded the Front trenches, support trenches and mine craters from 10-0 a.m. to 3-0 p.m. each day.

4.5" Howitzers bombarded FRANKS KEEP and RYANS KEEP and the trench joining them from 10-0 a.m. to 4-0 p.m. daily.

18 Pdrs. enfiladed front and support trench on either flank of the area bombarded and all communication trenches leading to it during the bombardment and throughout the night of 28th-29th and part of the night of 29th-30th.

The shooting of the heavy howitzers was somewhat interrupted on the 28th by enemy aeroplanes which could not be driven away. The shooting generally speaking was very good and great damage was done to the German line, large quantities of timber, sand-bags, etc., going up in the air. It is not possible to estimate the damage done to the mining works.

There was little retaliation on the 28th, but a good deal on the 29th from field guns and howitzers up to 5.9".

R.A., 2nd Divn.
30-11-1915.

Brigadier-General,
C.R.A.,   2nd Division.

"A" Form. Army Form C. 2121.
MESSAGES AND SIGNALS.

| TO | Z Group | A Group |

Sender's Number.	Day of Month.	In reply to Number	AAA
M 923	30		

One gun 7 Mountain Battery now in action with you is placed at disposal of A Group and addressed Z Group repeated A Group

From: Rawson
Place:
Time: 11.15 am

B.M.935.

Headquarters,
    2nd Division.

With reference to 2nd Divn.G.S.681/10, I submit the following :-

(9). 9.2")   On enclosed work.
      8"   )   1 hour   100 rounds.

      4.5"   Communication trench from junction
               A.11.c.4.5 to enclosed work.
               Communication trench from enclosed work
               to canal.
               1 hour   120 rounds.

      18-pdrs. PLAIN ALLEY.   TOWPATH ALLEY.
      H.E.   1 hour   200 rounds H.E.

(10). 9.2")   Front line trench from CANAL to A.16.a.2.9.
      8"   )   30 minutes   50 rounds.

      6"   TORTOISE.   30 minutes   50 rounds.

      4.5"   Front line trench A.9.d.8.2 to A.16.a.2.9.
               30 minutes   50 rounds.

      18-pdrs. On 4 Communication trenches 120 rounds.H.E.
               On line of water trench 200 rounds Shrapnel.

(11).(PLUME HOUSE).

      6"Hows. 50 rounds or as much as required to
               destroy the house.

      18-pdr. 100 rounds shrapnel to search ground in
               East of house during bombardment.
               1 hour.

(12). 9.2")   On railway work.
      8"   )   30 minutes   50 rounds.

      6"   Small work A.27.b.9.5.   50 rounds.

      4.5"   Front trench from MINE ALLEY to AUCHY
               ALLEY where not engaged by heavy howitzers
               and support trench.   120 rounds.

      18-pdrs. MINE ALLEY, TRAIN ALLEY, AUCHY ALLEY.
               150 rounds H.E.

(13)) To be done simultaneously.
) 8" Hows.   60 rounds on the Keeps.
(14).) 4.5" —   100 rounds on trench joining Keeps.
         18-pdrs. 200 rounds H.E. on communication
                   trenches, leading to Keeps.
                   About 1 hour.

Also proposed -
(A). Work near LONE FARM A.28.b.10.5.

      9.2")   On Work.
      8"   )   30 minutes   50 rounds.

      18-pdrs. 100 rounds H.E.   MINE ALLEY and
               CEMETERY ALLEY.

                                            ...Bvr.

(B). House on HAISNES ROAD A.30.c.7.2.

    60-pdr. as required.

Bombardments to be carried out in the following order:-
(12) (A) (11), (9), (13 & 14), (10), (B).

R.A., 2nd Divn.
30-11-1915.

Brigadier-General,
G.R.A., 2nd Division.

LIST OF OFFICERS. R.A., 2nd Division.

Headquarters. -
- Brigadier-General G.H.Sanders, D.S.O. — G.O.C., R.A.
- Major J.L.Mowbray, D.S.O. — Brigade Major.
- Captain L.G.Buxton, M.V.O. — Staff Captain.
- 2nd Lieutenant R.Scott. — A.D.C., to G.O.C., R.A.

34th Brigade.
Lt.Colonel C.R.P.Parry.
Lieut. A.A.M.Durand. (Adjt).
2/Lieut. B.Miles.

50th Battery.
Captain J.A.Don.
" W.E.Maitland Dougal, D.S.O.
Lieut. A.T.Sloan.
" P.G.Bailey.
2/Lieut. A.Heads.
" E.J.P.Stevenson.
" F.W.Flynn.

70th Battery.
Major W.A.F.Jones.
Capt. I.C.Pery Knox Gore.
Lieut. T.J.Moss,
" G.Lorimer.
2/Lieut. H.S.Perry.
" J.J.Sherman.

34th B.A.Column.
Captain M.W.G.Corrie. (Sick leave).
2/Lieut. W.J.S.Baird.

36th Brigade.
Lt.Colonel H.D.O.Ward.
Lieut. B.B.Quiller Couch. (Adjt).
T/2/Lieut. B.B.Murdoch.

15th Battery.
Captain R.L.Palmer.
" B.L.Marriner.
Lieut. S.K.Thorburn.
2/Lieut. G.F.Claudet.
" W.H.Manifold.
" R.G.Oakley.

48th Battery.
Captain H.F.Grant-Suttie.
" A.L.P.Griffith, D.S.O.
Lieut. S.A.Kellagher.
2/Lieut. G.A.Hoyland.
" F.S.Siggers.
" E.W.Manifold.

71st Battery.
Major R.ff.Powell.
Lieut. F.L.V.Mills.
" E.G.Barkham.
" V.Walrond.
2/Lieut. R.Q.Thomas.
T/2/Lieut. A.N.Dickson.

36th B.A.Column.
T/Capt. T.H.Fletcher. (Sick).

36th B.A.C(contd.)
Captain A.Anderson Pelham.
2/Lieut. A.C.Lutyens.
T/2nd/Lt. F.L.Wallis.

41st Brigade.
Lt.Col. E.W.M.Powell, D.S.O.
Lieut. F.J.R.Rodd. (Adjutant).
2/Lieut. L.L.Reeves.

9th Battery.
Captain H.G.Lee Warner, D.S.O.
Lieut. H.Lowe.
" C.H.Putnam.
2/Lieut. H.Martin.
" J.W.Sidley.
Captain E.G.L.Cullum. (attd).

16th Battery.
Major C.D.G.Lyon.
Captain S.Atkinson.
Lieut. G.Messervy.
2/Lieut. E.G.Audland.
" E.A.J.Wright.
" G.A.Scott.

17th Battery.
Major H.H.Joll.
Captain D.C.Stephenson.
Lieut. A.J.Wark.
2/Lieut. L.G.Sandford.
" J.J.Armitage.
" W.C.Stirrup.

41st B.A.Column.
Captain R.Fernie.
Lieut. O.Gaunt.
2/Lieut. C.H.N.Young.
" A.L.Kershaw.

44th Brigade.
Lt.Colonel E.H.Harpur.
Lieut. H.E.Barkworth. (Adjt).

47th Battery.
Major T.N.French.
Lieut. H.Cutbush. (Hospital).
Lieut. P.S.Fraser-Tytler.
2/Lt. R.T.Baxter.
" G.T.Taylor.
" C.L.Greig.

56th Battery.
Major B.B.Crozier, D.S.O.
Capt. H.F.Willcocks.
Lieut. W.H.Brookes.
" W.G.Dyson.

(P.T.O.

56th Battery.(Contd).
T/Lieut. D.F.Anderson.
2/Lieut. A.J.Shipley.
" J.M.Sanger.

44th B.A.Column.
Capt. A.D.Le Sueur.
2/Lieut. B.W.Stubbs.

Div.Ammn.Column.
Br.Colonel A.Eardley Wilmot.
2/Lieut.W.M.Drake.

No.1 Section.
T/Major E.W.Cushen.
Lieut. C.F.Wilkins.
2/Lt. W.O'Brien.

No.2 Section.
Lieut. W.Mellors.
2/Lt.T.O.Boyd.
Lieut. H.E.Courage.

No.3 Section.
Captain E.W.Griffith.
Lieut.A.Anderson Pelham.(Tempy.Comdg.36th B.A.C.).
Lieut. F.W.Sabine.
2/Lieut.C.H.Weston.

Territorial Officers Attached.
Major G.C.Peake.   50th Battery.
Capt. C.F.Benyon.   50th   "
 "   F.E.C.Stanley.   70th   "
 "   G.H.Jones.   70th   "

1536

DAILY AMMUNITION RETURN

DATE 30. XI. 1915

BATTERIES.

Piece	Projectile	Code	50	70	15	48	71	9	16	17	47	56	Total	Per Piece
18-pr	Guns......		6	6	6	6	6	6	6	6	6	6		
	Shrapnel...	"A"	36	20	249	159	56	16	129	22	—	—	687	
	H. E......	"Ax"	9	24	57	79	16	54	6	281	—	—	526	
4.5"	Howitzers..										—	—	—	
	Shrapnel...	"B"									—	—	—	
	H. E......	"Bx"									62	146	208	

www.ingramcontent.com/pod-product-compliance
Lightning Source LLC
Chambersburg PA
CBHW080853230426
43662CB00013B/2095